6 Rabbit Holes of Leadership

Six key ways you are unknowingly killing your business & career

K.W. Wrede

K.W. Wrede

Copyright © 2016 K.W. Wrede

Edition 0

ISBN-13: 978-0692783115
ISBN-10: 0692783113

Profitability Leadership LLC

Cover art by Jonathan Pritchard

PRAISE FOR
6 RABBIT HOLES OF LEADERSHIP

"One of the problems of being an entrepreneur and small business owner is that everything you do, you accomplish alone. Leadership questions are hard to articulate and you hope you don't make any fatal mistakes. The information and reasoning from this book and the idea of starting at the end really helped me to see what I did right and when I went wrong. After growing to five stores, I know I have done pretty well, but it is a relief to have the confirmation from the EndGame philosophies. I worry less about my leadership style and focus on a good corporate culture for my employees."

John Neville, Managing Director
Neville Jewellers, Cork, Ireland

"I have been in the aerospace industry for 15 years. Before reading Ken's book I spent a lot of time putting a lot of pressure on myself to be a good leader. It was exhausting. I often received feedback that I was being too hard on myself and to try to relax.

From the book and the EndGame Leadership way of looking at leadership, I learned that there was no recipe to be a good leader. You just have to be yourself and focus on business. The simplest things are often the best and the most effective.

Thanks to this new mindset, I saw a clear change in my environment and in my job. But is wasn't just me, other people were really opened up and became willing to work with me.

Within couple of months, I achieved many of my professional goals and objectives. My boss gave me very positive feedback. I feel more confident and stronger; I am confident I am doing the right thing.

I feel more like a better leader every day."

Laurent Savary, Airbus, France

"I am relatively new to the leadership game and its practical applications. I received my Bacholer's in Business in Management/Leadership, which gave me a strong academic background from my College, but the theory did not wholly prepare me for the real world.

Ken Wrede's EndGame Leadership approach has given me a sense of ease with its honest, in-depth framework. As a new leader, it has been hard to determine what effective leadership is based on the examples in my limited work experience. After reading Ken's "6 Rabbit Holes of Leadership" and better understanding the EndGame Leadership model, I have a better comprehension of leadership and what makes a good leader.

It wasn't just me not "getting it".

Perhaps I cannot change the people I work with, but I now understand bad-good-great leadership when I see it. Since I now know great leadership, I will be a great boss and leader for my people now and into the future."

Ashley Eamer, HR Professional
Tampa, Florida, USA

"Ken Wrede has a vast experience in global leadership. Any leader, entrepreneur or investor is wise to listen to his insights."
Loren Murfield, Ph.D. CEO of PWRuniversity.com

DEDICATION

This book is dedicated to those people who have lost endless nights of sleep worrying about their people and their organization. I am you.

It is for those entrepreneurs and geeks who were suddenly thrust into positions of leadership but had no clue how to start. I was you.

It is for senior leaders who worry about the future and survival of their organizations – how will it survive in your absence? I have been you.

This dedication is both personal and abstract.

From the personal side, this book is dedicated to those I've been able to help and to those I have failed. To those I've failed, I accept the full responsibility. Any failure was probably due to my ignorance, inexperience, or some combination thereof. To those I've helped, I hope you use your knowledge to avoid my mistakes and to help others to succeed.

In the more abstract - this book is for those who are strangers to me, but who I know will soon be introduced to their coming leadership challenges and the satisfaction it brings when things go right. If this saves you any time and helps you avoid the common pitfalls in the pursuit of your mastery, it will have served my intended purpose.

For those who are more experienced business leaders, I hope this book helps you to diagnose problems you've experienced, but just couldn't put your finger on. I further hope that it gives you the vocabulary to express your lessons-learned to those you lead or mentor. Your primary goal should not be to cultivate their loyalty, but to help them become successful.

Loyalty will follow on its own.

Let's face it, you are on a countdown. If leadership is a weak skill, it is only a matter of time before it creates a problem or business failure.

Contact me and/or follow me at my website: www.EndgameLeadership.com.

Let's accelerate your learning curve and eliminate the dangers that poor leadership creates.

Table of Contents

ACKNOWLEDGMENTS

First, I wish to acknowledge and thank Lieutenant General Bruce R. Harris US Army (ret) who, I suppose, recognized some small spark of potential in me and gave me the opportunity to observe his endgame leadership accomplishments first hand. Maybe it was hard to tell at the time, but I was listening and learning from you each day.

Thanks to my wife Carol. Thank you first and foremost for your patience, but also, for sharing your leadership experience and insights from over an amazing 32 years of federal service at the Senior Executive Service (SES) level.

I started my leadership path in September of 1977. Thank you Charles J. Farrell, Major, US Army (ret) for that first class "Military Science 101 (MS101) in 1977." Thanks even more for showing me that humor is a necessity in challenging times. Great leaders need to have the confidence to take that humor, turn it around and laugh at themselves.

It is almost impossible to express my thanks to so many people for so many insights, but I would be remiss if I did not include the Class of 2014 from the HEC EBMA Paris (École des Hautes Études Commerciales d'Paris, Executive MBA) program. It was not just the first-class, formal instruction, but the amazing, world-class experiences shared by my classmates. I learned something new from each of you.

Thanks also to the class delegates who helped me wrangle the class and create a class culture that has been the envy of past and current classes. I am talking to you Kim Do, Petra Muehlhaus, Laurent De Gregorio, and Shadi Nekavand. You made us legend.

A special mention to Jonathan Pritchard of A Life Well Designed. Although I try to be a sort of mentor to you, I think I have actually learned more from you than vice versa. Your practical sense and artist's eye have been invaluable in many ways.

Dorie Clark, speaker and author of "Reinventing You," lit this fuse by telling me I had something to say. Thanks Dorie, I am now saying it.

Dr. Michael McDermot and Dr. Luc Wathieu from the Georgetown University McDonough School of Business have been, perhaps unwittingly, immensely helpful. Your generous time and honest advice led me along this path.

For help in navigating my new home area, sincere thanks to Irene Hurst (director of the MBA and Executive MBA programs at University of South Florida's Muma College of Business), Matt Michini, and Sydney Manderson (both of Michini Wealth Management), Laurie MacDonald (MacDonald Consultants) and Alan Gorlick (Gorlick Financial Strategies). Each of you have been generous and kind in the opening of doors.

One of my unexpected joys has been to meet and learn from a few fantastic guys: Gil Effron (Profitability Institute), Tom Panaggio (The Risk Advantage), and Joe Yazbeck (Prestige Leadership Advisors). Thank you for your generosity and for that highly valued quality - honesty.

Any success I achieve is in many ways thanks to your contribution.

Any errors you notice, from past or present, I claim as my own.

INTRODUCTION

This book is laid out in two parts and nine chapters. Each chapter is self-standing, and based upon articles from my blog at EndGameLeadership.com.

My hope is to engage you in the same lifelong conversation I have been having. The difference is, I have been talking to myself.

If you have a comment or a story, please contact me directly at:

ken@endgameleadership.com.

Please share a story or experience; let me know if this book was of any help.

I'd love to hear from you.

As earlier mentioned, the book is organized into two parts to separate my thoughts and musings from the more practical information.

Part 1 is comprised of three chapters that are more philosophical. I hope to show you the intention of my thought processes - where I'm coming from, so to speak. I am leaning on the old adage of teaching you to fish instead of giving you a fish. I am not concerned so much with "what" you think, but I hope to influence "how" you think; in a critical, logical way.

Part 2 is comprised of six chapters - six rabbit holes. They are the result of a loose collection of experiences and conversations I have had with other leaders and would be leaders over the years. It was the repetition of the experiences and outcomes of those events that convinced me of the ubiquity of the pitfalls of leadership. Let me help you to avoid those rabbit holes and the consequential waste of time.

The truth of real rabbit holes is that they are a complex system of winding tunnels that lead to chambers and multiple entrances.

Rabbits cannot teleport, it just seems that way.

In real life, there are two ways rabbit hole will confound

you.

First, if a predator chases a rabbit to the entrance hole, it can wait there forever hoping to ambush that rascally rabbit. Other exits, remember?

You wait. And, you wait. And… you get nothing.

Second, a more industrious predator might start digging into the hole or explore the tunnels to chase down that rascally rabbit. The tunnels are long, the ways are many, and, once again, other exits.

You dig. You run blindly in the dark. You get nothing.

For whatever reason you focus on a rabbit hole, you are wasting your time.

I refer you to the famous animated documentary series: "Bugs Bunny."

Part 1: Starting at the end

"Begin with the end in mind."
                    ~ Steven Covey

"You know what the bad endings are, avoid them.
This isn't a slasher movie.
>   *Stay out of the basement.*
>   *Don't go to the attic.*
>   *Don't get into the van."*
                    ~ K. W. Wrede

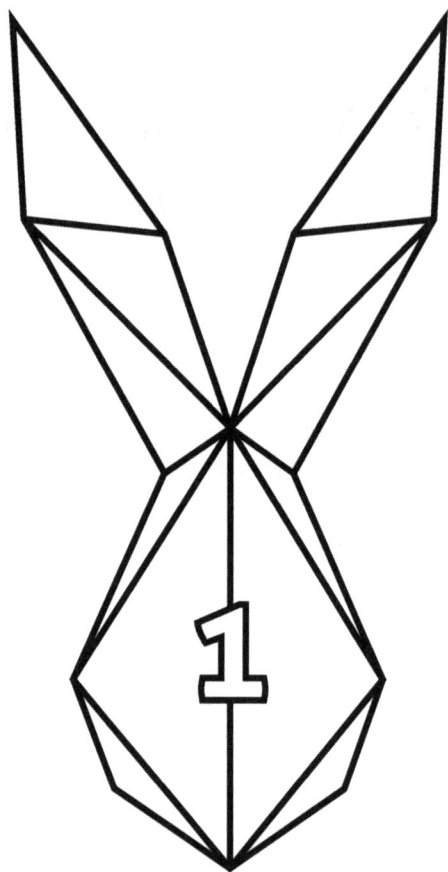

"Good judgement comes from experience, and a lot of that comes from bad judgement."
~ **Will Rodgers**

Chapter 1: The Right Road

My leadership path started in 1977 with my first leadership class from Army ROTC. I'll admit, it sounds a little ostentatious, an 18 year-old kid taking a military college class on how to lead others. But, everyone has to start sometime and start somewhere. My start was in that class.

I am nobody special, a person of normal potential and merit.

However, if there was one trait I have always tried to cultivate it was to try to be brutally honest with myself and self-aware of both my faults and talents.

That honesty with myself, especially in those challenging and private times, is my biggest strength. I am happy to share my mistakes and missteps if there is a chance you will be able to avoid them.

So, if we fast-forward four years from that first class, you would have seen a skinny, bespectacled Army second lieutenant with shiny new gold bars on his way to his first duty station, full of mission, pride, and a sense of purpose.

After my fourth or fifth trip to the county jail to visit or retrieve one of my soldiers from the hoosegow, you can imagine that my thoughts were along the lines of "What the hell did I get myself into?"

There is no yellow brick road

There are many roads to leadership, but no right road to follow.

Everyone has their own road and it is a solitary one of trial and error. Because each person is so caught up within the blinders that is their personal perspective, one and all make the same mistakes over and over again: the same rookie mistakes, the same middle manager mistakes, the same senior manager mistakes, the same executive level mistakes.

We are not perfect, so making mistakes in leadership is normally unavoidable and, in many ways, the errors are the equalizer for everyone. The right road does not exist because everyone's journey is deeply personal. Hopefully, they survive their mistakes or if they are lucky, they learned something along one of the easy pathways:

Easy pathways like:

1. The mistake was not critical enough to harm any person or the organization...

   but, lessons learned.

2. The organization recognized the fallibility of people, mitigated potential risk, and tolerated reasonable errors...

   but, lessons learned.

3. The mistake was made by someone else so that you could learn by observation...

   but, lesson learned.

4. You had a mentor that guided you and, perhaps, protected you from your errors...

   but, lessons learned.

5. If you were extremely lucky, you actually received leadership training...

   Lessons learned - avoid potential problems

The common thread in the first four points above is that the mistake happened first and everyone hoped that the mistake's impact was not serious enough to harm others, harm the organization, or lose their jobs.

So, the obvious, most utilitarian approach to leadership is training. Unfortunately, it is so hard to prioritize the different aspects of leadership. The breadth of skills is wide. What is the most important action (or actions) you need to take as a leader? What will have the greatest impact in exchange for effort and resources spent?

Is wisdom experience or just context?

As I mentioned before, I took my first formal leadership course when I was 18 years old. I remember opening the text book with a feeling of anticipation. I thought I was opening a kind of magic book that would reveal to me the secrets to motivate and control other people. It was full of definitions, leadership principles, leadership styles, leadership qualities, and pillars of leadership - a smorgasbord of leadership stuff.

At the time, it all made sense and it all seemed important. But, the one thing that was missing - was context. You can learn from war stories and anecdotes, but it seems that the best way we can acquire context is through experience. Even with the training, we end up right back on the experience train - hoping that we learn fast enough not to fall off.

Fast forward again to my last leadership course.

This time, I had almost 40 years of context. Context in the military, civilian businesses, startup companies, and federal government agencies. Context by living in the cultures of five different countries, and working in a half score of different countries. Beaucoup context.

Pass it along

My early experiences in the Army gave me a lot of contexts. Let me share a little.

My era was just post-Vietnam war. The US pulled out of Vietnam in April 1975, but the experience was still fresh in the national consciousness. Unlike today, being in the military was not a source of national pride. Wearing my uniform while traveling could equally get me a handshake or a spirited comment or a spit in the eye. It was a time when the judicial system still gave potential career criminals the choice: the Army or jail. Some of my guys chose both. They were the guys I usually visited in jail, the other jailbirds were my knuckleheads. The knuckleheads went to jail because of poor judgment or timing - the usual for any population cross-section.

I can't say I was miserable; there was no reason to pity me. I was having a great time in my new career. However, I will say that the best leadership training program in the world did not prepare me for my experience, it did not give me the tools to troubleshoot the situation and find the root cause.

I could not have articulated that nuance back then, but with context I can now say that the important point I learned was you cannot lead people who do not want to be led. It showed me that even in the military there were people who resisted authority. If that was true in such a highly structured place, it was more likely to be true in other areas.

That experience at that moment in my life was valuable and did teach me a few things. It taught me, eventually, that a systemic approach to leadership can identify and resolve leadership problems, not pass them along to the next person.

Passing the buck sergeant

For example, back in my first unit, we had one Sergeant (E5) who was a total screw-up. I don't care where you are from or your professional background, you all know someone like this guy - everybody has a person or two like him in their lives.

He wasn't a criminal screw-up, but he could not supervise the soldiers who worked for him. If there was one thing you could count on, it was that in three or four months he would screw up. When he did screw up, it was in such a way that the younger soldiers could no longer respect him. So, we moved him on to the next platoon, and later all the platoons in our company - then, the next company and, eventually, all their platoons - then the next battalion and a few of their platoons. The long story short, after three years of this, he was promoted.

How?

How was this possible? In those three years, he was never in a place long enough to qualify for a performance evaluation. In the absence of proof of poor performance, the promotion board had no choice but to promote.

I promised myself that, whenever it was in my power, I would never pass a problem on to others. My contribution to the system was to identify any problem and either fix it or, in the case of soldiers, rehabilitate or remove them.

... we are destined to repeat them

Back to my most recent class - here is the surprising, sort of sad part - the leadership class I took in 2014 was basically the same as the class I took in 1977. The conversation, in my mind, had not progressed at all.

Almost 40 years later, and the path forward is still solitary and everyone seems still destined to make the same mistakes as their predecessors. How can we break the cycle of risk and failure in leadership?

My humble goal with this book is not to give you a comprehensive course in leadership. My goal is to introduce you to a new, fundamental model of leadership and give you a way forward. Focus on the final result you want, then prioritize everything else toward that end.

Don't look at leadership from your personal and professional development. Don't view the result from your perspective and your success as a leader. Look at it from the view of the organization. Will the organization thrive? Will the organization even survive?

I started this conversation with the line, "There are many roads to leadership, but no right road to follow." You can succeed as a leader, eventually, given enough time and experience.

There are, however, *a lot* of wrong paths, paths that each seems compelling. They are compelling because they seem to resonate with us emotionally or they sound right because they remind us of a story or adage we heard before. These paths are the traps. They are the time killers or rabbit holes. In more contemporary terms, they are the cat videos of leadership development. They seem mesmerizing, but add zero value to leadership training or development. In fact, worse than giving zero value, they waste your time like endless cat videos and misdirect your attention.

Follow the evidence

My overall purpose is to introduce you to an evidence-based approach to leadership. An evidence-based approach focuses on studies and research that suggests the best and most effective means of developing leadership skills and, in so doing, being a good leader. If you concern yourself with only an ideology of leadership, you build a foundation on opinion. You must instead, follow the solid evidence to its reasoned conclusion.

> *"Science follows evidence to support a conclusion; ideology starts with a conclusion and seeks evidence to prove it."*
> *~ K. W. Wrede*

We cannot predict the precise efficacy of leadership training except to say we will fail without it. So, instead of supposing a list of skills that may or may not make you into a good leader, let us reexamine the problem from the other end. We can ask what companies failed because of leadership problems and what were the root causes of those problems?

I call this approach Endgame Leadership. This is not

one of those Zenish platitudes from a Matrix movie - I don't want you to visualize and "be the spoon." I don't want you to visualize a happy, successful ending and hope that is enough. This is not an exercise in wishful thinking.

The endgame implies that you focus on the end result. By reviewing the massive data of leadership failures, we can draw systemic conclusions about how to prevent these failures from happening. View the end and identify how to avoid the processes and behaviors that cause bad outcomes and encourage the processes and behaviors that cause good outcomes.

Abraham Wald: The Essence of EndGame Leadership

Abraham Wald is responsible for saving hundreds, if not thousands, of American and Allied airmen from World War II until present day - and you have probably never heard of him.

Wald was born in Austria-Hungary (present day Romania) in 1902 and immigrated to the US in 1938 after Germany invaded his homeland. Considered a genius even among his peers, he spent World War II working for the Statistical Research Group (SRG), a strategic think tank working on behalf of the Department of War.

In the words of W. Allen Wallis, the director of the SRG, the SRG was "the most extraordinary group of statisticians ever organized, taking into account both number and quality."

The military one day approached the SRG and posed the question to Wald: what is the optimum way to protect aircraft with armor?

The basic modes of defense are as old as war. Each mode, basically armor and mobility, trades off between their inherent advantages and disadvantages. With no armor, you are vulnerable but more maneuverable. Too much armor and your additional protection makes you slower and less agile. Adding to the complexity of air warfare - armor equals weight, weight increases fuel consumption, higher fuel consumption means less range.

The military collected after action damage reports on every returning aircraft with the following statistics:

Number of bullet holes per square foot

Engine: 1.11
Fuselage: 1.73
Fuel system: 1.55
Rest of plane: 1.8

Based on this information, what would you recommend?

Wald's recommendation was armor where the bullets aren't: the engines.

Wald's contribution was to understand that given an even distribution of bullet holes across all planes, the planes with the most catastrophic bullet holes were the ones that never returned. Wald asked, where are the missing bullets? Answer: with the missing planes.

The unspoken assumption of the officers presenting the information to Wald was that the data set was complete with a random distribution of bullet holes. Wald stepped back and asked what are the assumptions and are they valid?

The term survivor bias refers to the concept that you only count the data that you have at hand. After a catastrophe, what is left and what is missing?

Abraham Wald's story is the essence of Endgame Leadership. If you focus only on the data that is left, your story is incomplete. EndGame leadership examines the missing bullet holes in failed businesses.

That is where we put the armor.

The missing bullet holes of leadership

Studies suggest that when leadership fails, it is because of one of the following reasons:

The leaders were:
1. Out of touch with the facts.
2. Did not understand stakeholder needs.

3. Created or tolerated an apathetic, at best, or toxic, at worst, work environment.
4. Could not respond effectively to a crisis or major change.

If those reasons are the specific causes of leadership failure, the endgame evidence suggests exactly the steps you need to take to avoid failure:

1. Be intellectually coherent
2. Understand the drivers to motivate others
3. Keep the organization healthy
4. Learn to anticipate crisis and survive

It may not be rocket science, but it is science.

For your consideration
- View leadership as a system of behaviors to drive profitability.
- Adopt an evidence-based approach to leadership as it is the way forward.
- Be brutally self-critical.
- Do not be physically or mentally absent.
- Protect healthy organizational culture.
- Plan for crisis.

I just saved you a lot of time, use it like this:
- Cultivate the habit of self-critique; this is not self-doubt. It is the habit of thinking critically about yourself, your situation, information, and other people.
  It is an honest assessment.
- Mistakes are lessons learned: Think of a time when all the information was there, but you did not pay attention.
- What would you have done differently?

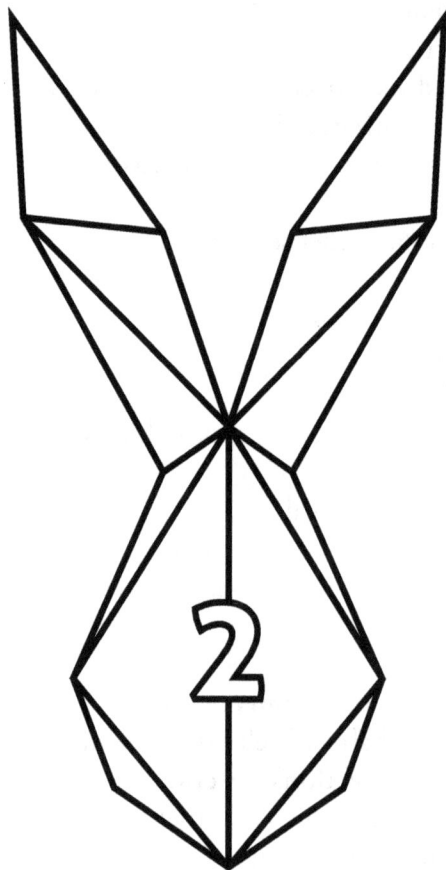

Chapter 2: The Fog of Leadership

The importance of leadership is so obvious to people that they often do not state it. In everyone's mind, they believe the other person knows exactly what they mean, so why bother? The vague reasoning and resulting vague conversations lead to vague goals and unpredictable outcomes.

Rookie mistakes can happen at any age

I worked with a guy who was, basically, a Donald Trump. That may sound ridiculous, but he exhibited many of the self-serving, narcissistic qualities that has made Donny Jingle so fascinating to observe in the media.

He was famous in our local area for accusing the government and the largest, incumbent player in our market of collusion or anti-competition plots. It sounded almost paranoid in the news interviews.

This guy was not incompetent. He was intelligent, and an amazing sales guy but his commitment to leadership was zero. If I had to qualify his style, it was that he was a cult leader in training. Our staff was expected to be loyal to him, not to the company - in fact, in his mind, he was the company. Loyalty to him was the preferred way to show loyalty to the company.

That fundamental difference in philosophy brought us into frequent conflict. The main problem, from my point of view, was to explain his conduct to the employees without condoning it.

I bring this point up because leadership is a default, reflexive, foundational concern to me. For him, it was completely off of his radar. It became my self-assigned mission and responsibility to protect the staff from what I considered an erratic person.

The most important feature of that period was one that I have seen repeated time and time again in countless entrepreneurial situations: this company was his first real leadership position.

He was in his 40s, and I am sure he headed a team or two in his career, but he had never had the leadership experience of a large scale organization.

I don't care about your age or maturity, the day you start in your first leadership position is the day you are eligible for the rookie errors. Everyone makes them. Your best, early defense is to be aware of potential traps and work to minimize the damage.

The different angles of leadership

The discussion of leadership usually leans toward the business community. Most examples in this book will also be from business, but I specifically use the word "organization." A strong leadership model should be applicable to any organization, not just business. Most examples are related to business because basic research exists that can easily find numbers to measure success in terms of turnover, profits, and longevity. It is like Abraham Wald all over again, we tend to examine the simple, easy to find data.

Let's examine three points of view:
1. The organizational view
2. The potential leaders view
3. My personal view

The Value of Strategic Leadership

From an organizational point of view, leadership is a strategic resource to every organization. Ask any CEO or MBA student.

Studies show that:
1. Leadership problems are the direct cause of failure in 25% of all companies that go under in the first 5 years of existence.
2. Leadership problems reduce the net margin from 1% to 3%, which directly causes the destruction of corporate value.
3. CEOs who responded in a recent survey, stated that 70% rated their leadership development program from average to ineffective.

Everyone agrees that leadership is a strategic concern.

They know they should invest in any process that prevents their organization from going out of business or that increases corporate value. It is a no-brainer decision.

However, there is obviously a disconnection between a strategic concern and the implementation of effective leadership.

The critical question to ask is: where is the disconnect?

Another strategic organizational concern for any institution is what I call the "bus scenario." Is your organization prepared for worst case scenario? Is there someone suitable to assume key roles in the organization if a senior executive, or any leader at any level, were to be hit by a bus tomorrow? It seems like an unemotional approach, but many companies would be mortally wounded because there was no leadership succession plan or process in place. The smaller the organization, the greater the impact of a critical loss.

Nobody starts out to fail

The second point of view, potential leaders, rests with everyone who has ever held a leadership role. I begin from the fundamental premise of trust: no one starts out to become a poor leader and fail. This must be the assumption whether it is a person just beginning their journey, or an experienced executive. They want to personally succeed. They want the organization to be successful. The source problem may be that they can't get out of the way of their own egos.

Everyone has a natural proclivity level for leadership. Words are important here. I specifically use the word "proclivity" instead of "natural ability."

Leadership is teachable. Nevertheless, each person has their own starting point, which can make acquiring leadership skills easier or more difficult. If a person has no proclivity or inclination to lead, the road is harder.

In the same way good leadership skills can be learned, poor leadership behaviors can be ingrained. Poor leadership is mostly the result of learning from poor leadership examples, uncorrected bad habits, and/or an indifferent organization that does not correct adverse behavior.

Poor leaders often do not recognize the fact that they are poor leaders. There are a variety of mental blind spots that block their ability to see how their mental processes influences their behavior. There is actually a field of science that studies the causes and effects of blind spots called cognitive biases.

In general, cognitive bias studies show that there are internal and external processes that affect the way we assimilate, remember, and react to information. We can become so emotionally attached to the information we think we know and the conclusions we make that we will defend it all with the full power of our intellect and reason. Studies show that the stronger we are emotionally invested, the stronger we will defend our position even when presented hard, confirmed evidence. The sum effect and defense of all the biases is called cognitive dissonance.

Knowing that cognitive dissonance exists and can cloud your mind is reason enough to require an evidence-based, systemic approach to leadership. A rational approach can guide new leaders into effective leadership habits and expose, in an unbiased and non-accusatory manner, destructive leadership behaviors that must be corrected.

It is the responsibility of each organization to develop their leaders. In 2012, US companies spent $14 billion dollars on leadership training. Based on the money spent, there seems to be a good faith attempt by most to meet their responsibility. However, in view of the end result, the money is not spent effectively: year in and year out, leadership is still the primary reason for business failures.

My Personal Quest

Good leadership development is important for two reasons:

The first reason is that I hate the enormous waste of failed businesses due to unforced errors. About five million companies in the US will flop in their first five years because of bad leadership.

Five million!

If a company fails because of economic or market conditions, then that is part of a natural, Darwinian process. I want to prevent the failures that are the result of ignorance or egotistical leaders. If I could save just one company with effective leadership strategies, I have done my part.

I might just need a little help with the other 4,999,999 companies.

The second important reason, is that I hate bullies.

Everyone has some experience with bullies. Bullies

are people with a little bit of power who believe that their power is carte blanche to ignore all boundaries of acceptable social behavior. For example, encroaching on personal space, aggressive behavior, or an overdeveloped sense of entitlement. Unfortunately, some people believe that this dictatorial style of leadership is acceptable. Equally unfortunate, are the organizations that allow this kind of behavior because "it gets results."

I have witnessed so many organizations or departments destroyed by the egotistical, toxic behavior of self-proclaimed, "ass-kicking" leaders that I cannot keep count. The cost of lost productivity, personnel turnover, loss of operational continuity, and lost revenue is inexcusable. In what world do you motivate people by creating an environment of uncertainty, fear, and constant criticism? Yet, I have witnessed the same behavior from some of my bosses, coworkers, subordinates, and even clients. They excuse their behavior with their own honest belief that they are acting in a high-level leadership role which is "keeping people on their toes." They belong to the philosophical school of thought that believes that "fear is the same as respect." They don't know better.

There is nothing in leadership research that supports these opinions, but there is much research that specifically states that this behavior destroys corporate value and is directly attributable to organizational failures. When an organization allows toxic leadership, it undermines the foundation of the integrity of the organization and the relationships with their employees and, potentially, their customers. Most commonly, the behavior is excused as being an authoritarian leadership style. Research suggests that an authoritarian style is necessary and acceptable during crisis periods, but in the long-term, it is ineffective - even damaging - and will lead to high employee turnover and other negative outcomes.

It seems like every time I have spoken to anyone about toxic leaders, there is a universality of the experience. Everyone has either had a direct or indirect experience with a toxic boss.

The value of leadership is important on so many levels that its importance is acknowledged as a strategic postulation, but the value is never realized due to indifference or denial. Once everyone agrees that leadership is a prerequisite, their following concern should be developing it effectively.

Approaching leadership from the EndGame

My experience is that almost all leadership development programs are bottom-up driven - a loose series of classes.

The classes are intended to develop the individual management and leadership skills. I agree that these skills are important, but they should exist in a larger framework of a training strategy that builds toward the strategic endgame of organizational survival. Take for example juggling. Juggling is basically tossing an object in the air and catching it. But, those two skills hardly convey the gestalt and complexity of juggling.

The available resources of time and money should be spent on making the candidates into effective leaders.

For your consideration
- Own the personal responsibility of leadership
- Toxic leadership destroys company value.
  ### *Don't do it!*
  ### *Do not tolerate toxic behavior in others!*
- Approach leadership development as a system.
- Use an evidence based approach to leadership and create effective leaders.

I just saved you a lot of time, use it like this:
- Use the time to reflect on your past experiences in professional, social, and volunteer groups.
- As you think about any past or future leadership classes, think about them as tactics.
- Don't confuse tactics with strategy. Tactics are used in the

execution of strategy.

- Tactics are a fluid set of tools that you use based upon the circumstances as they unfold before you.
- Think about toxic bosses you have experienced directly and indirectly. Remember their actions and how they made you feel.
- Is that how you also want to make people feel?

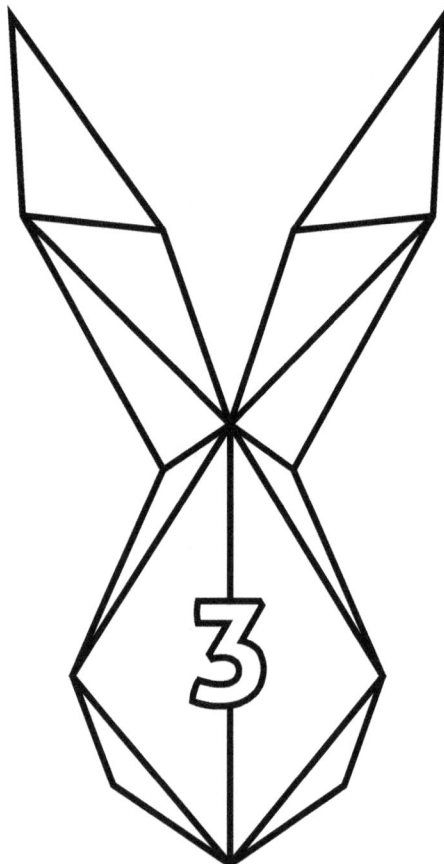

It must be true:
I read it on the Internet.
*~ **The Internet***

Chapter 3: Don't Say Eureka!

I want to inoculate you.

From the Internet.

A big undertaking, I know.

One of the biggest problems in any new endeavor is how to effectively allocate your time acquiring new information. You want to be efficient with your time, but it is often hard to prioritize or even to assess good information from bad. There are ways to separate the good evidence from the bad. However, instead of starting with the information quality, let's start with defending the receiver - you.

Like you, I am bombarded each day with articles, tips, and lists on leadership. They are interesting in a way; interesting in that the lists seem to satisfy that special emotion people cherish when they have the insider scoop on "information that will change their lives."

Fantastic!

But the fact is that the information's accumulative value is small, byproducts of a well-researched and well-understood psychological phenomenon known as "information bias."

It is well understood by marketing and sales people who use it to reinforce products and brands in advertising. It is what makes you a Pepsi person or a Coke person. I know I am not immune to the allure of these biases (Coke) and it takes a conscious effort to ignore the glitter and focus on an evidence-base truth.

(Coke Zero - there, I said it!)

The study of information bias suggests that the more frequent and more recent you hear something, the more you will believe it to be true - even if you know there is strong evidence that proves it is wrong. Your gut vetoes your brain.

This concept is widely known by everyone, but they still fall victim to its effect.

Your valuable time and your progress in leadership development are displaced by the captivating leadership equivalents: bathwater and "eureka!"

What does eureka even mean?

Displacement is one of those words that everyone knows. You can probably dredge it up from the distant mists of junior high school science classes.

What you remember from the class is probably something about bath water overflowing from a tub, Archimedes (the Greek dude, not the bird), and a vague mention about why we say "eureka."

The more complete and valuable story was that Archimedes was looking for a way to determine if gold was being fraudulently diluted with lighter, cheaper metals. Displacement was his solution.[1]

However, the compelling fable about the bath water and "eureka" completely hides the real value of the historical impact of the displacement story. Displacement is so important, it is called the Archimedes Principle and has become one of the foundational features of chemistry and physics.

More importantly in this example and the main reason I mention it is that the whole bathtub story probably never happened.

---

[1]   *"Fact or Fiction: Archimedes..." Scientific American, 28 December 2006,* *www.scientificamerican.com/aritcle/fact-or-fiction-archimede/*

The real lesson here is that displacement was itself displaced by a compelling yet fabricated story. The story became repeated so often that it is generally accepted as the truth. Facts were displaced by a commonly held, yet false, belief.

Displacement Makes You Fat

Displacement is common in other areas, for example in nutrition. Nutritional displacement is when we prefer to eat calorie-dense comfort food instead of nutritionally-dense food that, by all measures, is better for us.

We are lazy. This isn't a criticism, it is an observation efficiency. We'd rather dedicate only a minimum amount of time each day to food preparation and consumption, so we tend to go for fast and easy. In the US culture, fast and easy leans toward a high-carbohydrate, high-calorie diet. A person can eat full meals, but still not consume the proper balance of nutrients.

Nutrition is a complicated process, but again, displacement favors a questionable action over an optimum action at the expense of a more favorable outcome.

You need to learn to engage your massive, reasoning forebrain and ignore the insidious pressure of your lizard stem.

I present to you 6 rabbit holes for you to avoid - those captivating ideas that suck you in only to waste your time and energy. Recognize them for what they are and how each of them affects you. More broadly, I hope you begin to see the pattern behind them, then recognize and avoid similar rabbit holes in the wild.

For your consideration
- Follow the evidence.
- Challenge the commonly accepted wisdom of cliché. The danger of cliché is that we are wet-wired to react positively to things that sound familiar - even when they are wrong.
- Just because an aphorism feels right, does not make it true.

- For every aphorism, there is an equal and opposite aphorism that will seem just as compelling:

    "Nothing is more dangerous than an idea when you have only one idea."
    - Emile Auguste Chartier
    "If I have a thousand ideas and only one turns out to be good, I am satisfied."
    - Alfred Noble

I just saved you a lot of time, use it like this:

- Learn to recognize Red Flags:
    o The word "Secret" is in the title.
    o There is a list.
    o The solution to a complex problem is "both simple and easy."
- Take a systemic approach.
- Seek the strongest available evidence, draw conclusions from the evidence. Be prepared to change a weak conclusion based on weak evidence, when better evidence is revealed.
- Seek strategies and skills that will drive your organization forward and create a healthy organizational culture.
- Stay alert!
    Recognize the irrationality of compulsions. If something is compelling, take a step back and examine it. Your brain may just be fooling you.
- Then ask:
    Is it *really* true or does it make you *feel* as if it is *really* true?

Part 2: Into the Rabbit Holes

Alice: "How long is forever?
White Rabbit: "Sometimes, just one second."
~ Lewis Carroll, from
"Alice in Wonderland"

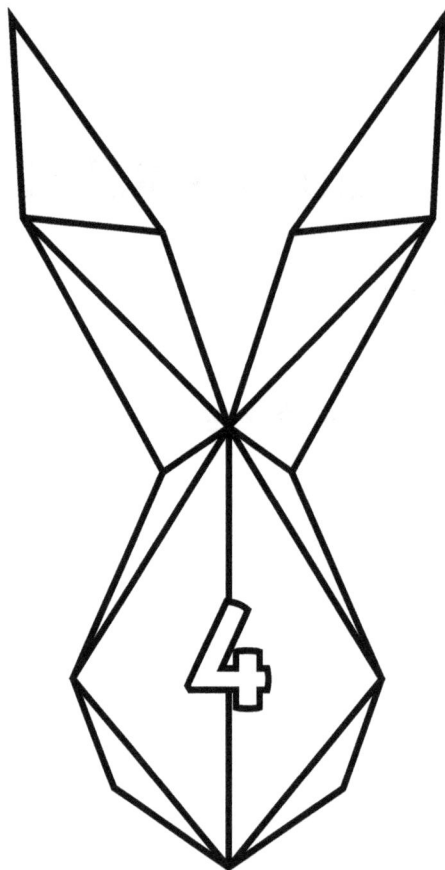

> *There is no guarantee that leadership will make*
> *an organization successful, but I can guarantee*
> *that without leadership, you're kinda screwed.*

~ *K. W. Wrede*

Chapter 4: The First Thing You Must Do

Rabbit Hole 1:
"You can run your business with only four hours each week."

The first and most important thing you must do as a leader is be present.

Show up.

Be there.

Be seen.

Interact with everyone.

A few years back, I had a strange conversation with an HR director about leadership and its role in the company. This person was an executive with 10-15 years of work experience and was strategically responsible for HR policy and recruiting. After the usual chitchat, I asked about the biggest leadership challenges the company faced (yeah, I'm the life of a party). Were there challenges of development or mentoring?

The HR director looked at me and said that there were no problems, "we don't use leadership in this company."

I don't like to use the word "gob-smacked" because it really doesn't suit me, but if ever there was a time to use it... that was it. I was pretty stunned. There was a bit of a pregnant pause while I processed that tidbit. I could not think of a way to continue without a few rude questions. Without both of us accepting the basic premise that all companies needed leadership, I had no way to move that conversation forward. So, I disengaged.

Luckily, there was a bar.

In some companies, there is no importance placed on leadership training. In smaller companies, leadership development and mentorship is minimal; if it exists at all. I understand completely that it can be a resource issue. It can be a drain on resources and not considered resource multiplier. The presence of the senior managers and their "bossness" is considered leadership enough.

Leadership is on autopilot. It is leadership is by example, and you have to hope that the example is a good one.

In transactional relationships, leadership is hard to force onto the workplace. The business relationship may be a simple trade of time and skills for an hourly wage. That is a fair observation. You can't force leadership principles on to a situation that requires management skills. It is an inappropriate use of leadership and it would feel insincere or inauthentic to the employees.

Leaderless

There are plenty of examples of people who grab the reins of power and squeeze as much out of it as they can. But, at the other end of the spectrum are people who react in a passive way to their position of power. Leadership is not exercised and the leader is disengaged or too inactive. They confuse the authority of their position (or being the boss) with leadership - they think power is sufficient on its own merit.

The cause of the disengagement or passivity is the would-be leader's reaction to having power and it can vary greatly:

- The person in position feels inadequate to the task of leadership and is reluctant to assume the authority and responsibility of power.
- The person in position has no experience, is overwhelmed, and does not know where to begin.

- The person in position thinks that if anybody needs guidance, they'll come and ask.
- The person in position assumes everything is good until it isn't.
- The person in position has no leadership support or mentorship from the level above.

So what does science suggest?

My definition of leadership is an operational definition that serves the leadership model, but it is derived from psychological and social evolutionary development tenets.

Many leadership definitions address the "why" of leadership (i.e.: to motivate others to a common goal), the functions of leadership, or leadership traits. I address the functional "how." What I mean is how the relationship between the leader and the follower is affected by evolved psychological factors and the evolutionary strategy of humans to survive as a group.

Biomass

Evolutionary theories suggest that one key strategy to survival is the accumulation of biomass. Biomass can be accumulated by developing into larger and more complex organisms (growth) or through more complex ecosystems (social development).[2]

Examples of physical growth can be seen in all ecological niches: lions, orcas, elephants, and whales. Examples of developmental growth can be seen in cell colonies from jellies to bison herds to socialized humans.

Of all the animals in existence, humans are some of the least suitable to survive alone in the wild. They are ill equipped for extreme weather, unarmed in terms of tooth and claw, and are not the fastest or the strongest. Regardless, humans are the planet's apex predator. The species had endured because

---

2   *A New Ecology: Systems Perspective (2007), P. 175, Sven Erik Jørgensen, Brian Fath, Simone Bastianoni, Joao C. Marque, Felix Muller, et al*

our survival strategy has been to accumulate biomass through close socialization. With socialization comes communication. Communication is the basis of small group organization.

Obedience

To avoid any confusion, obedience in this context is not a moral or cultural obligation to follow all orders from a person in authority. It refers to the social context related to group conformity and a deference to authority; an authority earned by social trust and confidence.

In their early lives, our ancestors probably surrendered authority to their parents in the same way we do to our parents: for personal protection and to learn about potential dangers in the world. As we developed the ability to communicate, it allowed us to express complex ideas and plans. There comes a time in every plan when during its execution, someone had to make a decision or give direction or say "ugh" (which means "go" in pre-modern humanity). Our prehistoric ancestors probably followed similar processes. Roles were defined and roles accepted: I lead and you follow.

Through communication and cooperation, our biomass became a tool we could use to herd larger animals into traps and keep other, more capable predators at bay.

From the flip side - leadership

Leadership cannot be imposed on unwilling followers. The obvious extreme of forced coercion is not leadership, but abuse of power.

A subordinate role can form in a prescribed hierarchy, in a social situation, in the presence of a knowledge expert, or in the presence of an authority figure. If a person accepts the subordinate role, a vacuum is created. To coordinate and accomplish some shared goal or task, another person must fill the leadership role.

As the leader, you must be there to fill that necessity. If

you do not fulfill that need, someone else will.

Let me give a quick, informal example. I sail occasionally with friends of mine. I would describe them as yachtsmen and yachtswomen based on their decades of experience on the water. But, for some reason, they hate talking on the radio. I'm not sure if they are embarrassed or just self-conscious, but they really dislike the experience. Since, I have a previous professional pride in my two-way skills, I step in as the designated radio guy. As I have mentioned before, a leadership role can be informal and fleeting.

The absence of leadership creates uncertainty and in that condition no one will want to risk making a bad decision on limited information. Subordinates will seek information in order to reduce uncertainty.

Being in a leadership role can be daunting, especially if it is your first experience. If a leader is passive or detached, the leadership can be unintentionally passed on to the next person in position or whoever accepts the role. The formal leader's risk is that an ad hoc leader may not share the formal leader's goals.

You could be interning your replacement.

So, science says that we are highly socialized animals that have developed our social skills as a survival strategy. We have been very successful. As a part of our evolutionary socialization some of us, in the interest of cooperation, assume the subordinate role and others filled the vacuum by assuming an authority role.

You cannot ignore the need for leadership. Leadership has been a natural evolutionary result as groups formed for our mutual survival. The groups needed a central figure for basic coordination at first, then grew as society became more complicated. Leadership is a response to fill a natural need for people to seek guidance and to reduce the feeling of uncertainty. The keys to fulfilling that desire are natural social skills everyone has: communication and empathy.

Just being there isn't enough

There is an adage, "Writers write."

The implied meaning of the adage is that there are people who claim to be writers, but do not actually do it. You need to write every day and practice your craft. It isn't enough to say you are a writer if your output is limited to jotting down story ideas. Ideas are great for a start, but the story and characters, or the technical manual has to be eventually written down.

Leaders lead. It isn't enough just to talk about it.

I know it can be daunting at first, but the most important part of leadership is engaging your staff through constant communication. You need to establish rapport and a relationship (perhaps your time limits you to a simple connection) with everyone. If for no other reason, it would be to encourage them to communicate with you.

For example, I was a coworker with a guy who supervised about ten people. It was his habit was to speak to almost nobody and to spend a lot of time in his office. He was lucky at first because he had another person in the office experienced enough and smart enough to keep the daily operation going.

In the morning, he went straight to his office barely speaking to anyone. In the evening, he went straight out the front door. The only time he spoke to his staff was to explain errors and criticize the quality of their work. He was diligent and very detail oriented. However, he placed as much emphasis on grammatical errors as he would on substance. Over time, the staff simply associated all communication with him as the next reprimand.

He never formally lost his job, but his position evaporated. The more experienced and smarter woman who gave him so much early support was promoted to a new department and took many of his staff and functions along with her. The rest of the staff either quit or arranged to have their functions moved to other departments. It became impossible to recruit internal replacements. He finally had to change companies because there was no work or workers left to supervise.

To this day, I am convinced that he did not understand the consequence of his actions and inactions on his final outcome.

Leaders must communicate to build trust. If every interaction is negative, employees have no reason to voluntarily communicate. It just becomes the next bad experience they have with their boss. In the "One Minute Manager," Ken Blanchard suggests that you try to catch your employees doing something right. It gives you an opportunity and reason to praise them.

I found this tactic as an easy and natural way for me to interact and engage with my subordinates. As I am trying to catch them doing something right, I am also better aware of their actions and behaviors. They become subtly aware of my attentions, the sum of which gives both sides reasons to communicate and develop mutual trust.

Listen

I supervised a team of people on 24/7 operations. I worked mostly, 9 to 5, but the rest had one of three rotating shifts: day, evening, and night.

The practical impact of the different work hours was that there was no way for me to see everyone only during my work schedule. Their schedule might eventually work back around to my normal hours, but it might take two or three weeks. If something was significant to them, I obviously couldn't wait that long. I had to sometimes come in at night and on week-ends to see them on their schedule.

The ad hoc conversations were as important to me as it was to them. During the bustle of daily operations, the work tempo or lack of privacy made a personal conversation impossible. But, everyone is the center of their own life. Sometimes, what may seem inconsequential or generic to us as leaders, might be keeping them awake at night.

If I could reduce the uncertainty or anxiety, it was better for them and the team. I cannot tell you how many times it took me an extra half hour to leave because someone started the conversation "Ken, can I ask you about something?" Because, unless there was a pressing matter for me, the answer was always "yes." A small detail I can fix now may prevent a big problem or misunderstanding later on down the road.

For your consideration
- "You can run your business with only four hours each week" should read "You can ruin your business with only four hours each week."
- Leadership is not an optional term.
- Accept on principle that leadership cannot be ignored.
- The emphasis on leadership has to be scaled to the size and nature of an organization.
- There are many reasons that leaders are absent, but none are acceptable as excuses.
- Leadership is a natural part of our social evolution. People expect to be led.
- To not actively lead while in the authority position is a breach of the social contract and may create unintended results.
- Open communication is the key to building trust. If employees know they can share bad news, you will be rarely and unexpectedly blindsided. You may not like the news, but you will be aware and can respond with solutions.
- Catch people doing something good.
  More importantly:
  Tell them! (Even better, say it in front of others.)
- Open communication is the key to building trust.
  (Yes, I know I am repeating this, but it is worth repeating.)

I just saved you a lot of time, use it like this:
- The most important takeaway is to disregard any book that tells you the shortcut to success is to ignore your responsibilities.
  There… I just saved you more time.

- It is a leader's responsibility to **earn the trust** of their subordinates. Leaders have **no right to demand** that trust.
- If you are not a touchy-feely person, I understand, but you still need to engage your people in a way that is natural. Start with the things you know. Start with the common social graces. Introduce yourself and make an effort to say "hello" and "goodbye" at those appropriate moments.
  If you ask people how they are, be prepared to stay and listen
- Many leaders are standoffish as a barrier to social interactions. Their reasoning is that they want to maintain a barrier between professional and personal behavior. It can set a bad tone for the workplace.
  Your professional and personal borderline should not be drawn at how you interact with people. That border is drawn along the line of your organizational health. If their behavior (or yours for that matter) has a negative impact on the health of the culture, then the professional line has been crossed.
  You can be kind and courteous without being overly familiar if it makes you uncomfortable.
- Manage by walking.
  Go out and see what the staff is doing. Catch them doing the good things. Get insights without filters. Let people see
- that you are interested and listening.
  This seems a good place to discuss delegating.
  I know that the impetus of the philosophy of "4 hours a week" is to emphasize delegating - which I agree is important. However, the absent, distracted boss still needs to be the leader.
  You may delegate the authority for the detailed work, but you still need to create and protect the most important asset generated by healthy organizational cultures:
  Trust.

K.W. Wrede

There is a balance, find it:
> Delegate too much and you lose control.
> Delegate too little, then you are probably micro-
> managing and stuck behind your desk all the time.

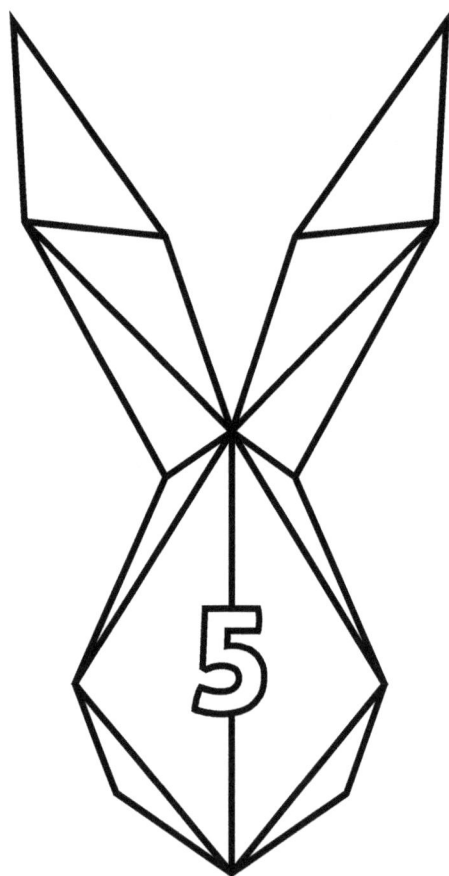

It gives you great abs!
~ **Clique Bate**

Chapter 5: The One Amazing *Secret* of Leadership

Rabbit Hole 2:
*It almost always begins: "I want to share with you the most important secret, the secret **they** do not want you to learn..."*

The biggest, most important secret of leadership...

The secret "they" don't want you to know...

The top item on every Internet list ever written about leadership is, and this is the key to your success...

THERE IS NO SECRET!!

If this was the Internet, 90% of you would have clicked the title of this chapter in hope of finally discovering the single most amazing secret. That sliver of hope, that optimism, is the power of clickbait for all lists ever presented on the Internet.

In 6 weeks...

If you asked the Internet, "How do I get great abs?" you would be bombarded with exercises and programs that promised a washboard stomach in 6 weeks. It would all seem logical and practical.

59

In your mind:

Exercise equals strength.

Strength equal Muscles.

So, exercise equals muscles, simple math.

But, what is truly the end result? After the promised weeks, would you really have great abs?

If you ask me the same question, first, I would ask, "What are your expectations? What are you willing to do to meet those expectations?" I would then find what the evidence says. Second, I would say, "Check your basic premise? Is exercise really the key? Will it create that trim, youthful waist line?"

From what we know about the science of muscle development, you cannot build up your abdominal muscles in such a way that they will stand out in relief from the backdrop of your abdominal wall. The abdominal muscles do not grow that way. Abdominal muscles are relatively short with a small cross section, so they even when become hypertrophic (bulging), the effect is relatively small and hardly noticeable. Exercise is useful to create strength and tone, but ab exercises alone will not cause great abs.

Unfortunately, the key to great abs is actually a little more complicated and difficult than people expect. That is something people never want to hear. Since the effort is long-term and requires a little more determination, it is difficult to get people to commit to the extra effort and the actual behavior that will be effective and give results. The key to great abs is something so obvious that you assume it is the byproduct of getting great abs, not the other way around.

The key is a low percentage of body fat. Competitive body builders compete at about 3% body fat. Fitness models are typically around 7-10% body fat.

It is the layer of fat just under your skin that hides the definition of your muscles. So, looking to the root cause of great abs, you have to attack the problem not from the muscle side, but from the component that covers the muscles - fat.

How do you approach reducing fat? My first suggestion is to select your parents very carefully... an old joke and I admit that I stole it. But, the joke illustrates that low body fat may be a natural condition as a result of the genetic lottery. Some people naturally have lower body fat. For those with a naturally higher percentage of body fat, they must begin from a more difficult starting point. My true suggestion to approaching the issue of fat is to modify your eating habits.

I specifically use the phrase "eating habits" instead of dieting because words are important. A diet implies a short-term behavior. "Modified eating habits" imply a change in lifestyle that would create a new norm of behavior. The intention of the new eating habits would be to eat in a manner that nourishes the machine, but does not encourage the body to store energy in the form of fat.

The compelling story of exercise includes very good-looking men and women who are textbook examples of the results in our minds. The story attracts us because the effort is within a limited timeframe (6 weeks) and with a limited amount of effort (whatever exercise program you selected). Everyone assumes they can do anything over a short period of time.

But, it is unlikely to produce the results in 98% of the attempted cases. To modify your eating habits requires planning, preparation, and a bit of self-discipline - boring!! Also, the timeframe is indefinite and possibly lifelong. This, however, is the method that will work.

Dreaming of great abs is the *real* secret
Not really.

People love compelling stories. The human mind is engaged by stories in two ways. First, a story creates an emotional resonance that gets us to care about a positive outcome (hyper-fit sports models) even if that outcome has no reflection in reality. Do you think sports models get hired because they already looked fantastic using the Amazing <Inset your favorite ab gimmick here>? Or, did they become fantastic looking because they used the Amazing <Inset your favorite ab gimmick here>? Our brains often have a problem with causality.

Second, we are evolutionally wired to make connections. It is a natural mental reflex to seek patterns and draw conclusions even if the patterns are constructs of our minds and not of real facts. Exercise seems to us to be the direct way to affect our abdominal muscles. Exercise has an irrefutable effect, but will not directly result in great abs.

Like great abs, leadership is also both simple and very complex. It is simple because once you accept the basic principles, you have a clear path to follow. It is complex because you have to execute consistently day after day. Your daily actions cumulate for a strategic benefit.

The non-leader non-option

Leadership begins with one simple rule, if you are in a position of responsibility over other people, leadership is not optional.

It might not feel like it, but leadership is a voluntary position. Within your own mind, you have to make the commitment to accept the responsibilities of leadership.

It seems as if the absent leader is another almost universal experience. Whenever I described the absent leader and asked the question, "Do you know a person like this?" almost everyone raised a hand.

A non-leader can be just as damaging as a "bad" leader - maybe even worse. It is the same as taking your hands off of the wheel of a car and closing your eyes. If you are lucky, perhaps the person in the seat next to you will control the wheel. Maybe a more competent right-seat passenger will control the wheel and whisper gas and brake instructions in your ear. Maybe you'll be lucky, and there will be a straight, wide section of road ahead with no obstacles. But, most likely, there will be obstacles and challenges. If you don't listen, the passengers will seek safe ways to get out of the car before the inevitable: you run off of the road, or it all ends in a fiery crash.

Leadership is mostly a broadcast relationship

What I mean by broadcast is that the relationship branches from one person to many people.

One level of complexity exists because, in the eyes of your subordinates, you occupy a dual-state relationship. Each of your subordinates perceives an individual, one-on-one relationship, even though you may rarely have conversations. Each person has the impression that the leaders is speaking to them directly even in a group. The feeling that others focus on you is a specific cognitive bias that everyone experiences called the "spotlight effect" which is the tendency for people to overestimate the detail that others notice in their appearance and behavior.

This is the same feeling one may experience by having a "friendship" with a favorite DJ or film celebrity; you really think you know them personally.

Leadership is also complex because it is an ongoing process. As a leader, you are always "on."

As a leader, you are always being evaluated by each individual; you are also being scrutinized by the aggregate group. In this case, this is not the spotlight effect; you are in the spotlight.

We love lists

The most difficult temptation of lists, secrets, tips, and strategies is that they seem incredibly plausible. They are captivating because they appeal to us on a visceral level through biases we all possess. First, is our tendency to seek patterns in almost everything: faces in burnt toast, the man in the moon, clouds shaped like animals, etc. A list is automatically and naturally perceived as a pattern. Second, on the level of social biases, collecting items appeals to us emotionally in a couple of ways: the anticipation or thrill of the hunt and the satisfaction of collecting. Some psychologists suggest these behaviors are related to our social wiring to gather food for survival. The group rewarded those who could better, recognize the pattern of edible plants and who gathered the most food.

Resistance is not futile; it is necessary

Resist questing for the perfect list or the best secret; your best action is to focus on the activities that truly lead to results. I illustrate these urges so that you can recognize them. These compulsions are such an intimate part of the way we perceive and think that we don't see them until we have to look for them. They are not a consequence of reasoned thought.

I know I am not immune to compulsions. It is a constant struggle and I continuously evaluate myself. I want to recognize the compulsion and ask myself, "What is the catch?" And, "What is the real story here?"

You must engage your brain, ask the same questions, and think: "what is a better use of my resources?"

There is one argument that I hope will convince you; a question to pose to yourself. As you read a "magical" list, ask yourself "Will this list predict my success or failure?" If you are already doing everything on the list, what is the outcome? Are you truly a great leader or does the list just make you feel good?

Be aware of the limits of lists and the sources. The echo chamber of the Internet tends to reinforce platitudes and aphorisms because they feel "right," but they are not the foundation of leadership.

For your consideration
- Leadership is not optional. Be present and be engaged.
- You are always on, act accordingly.
- If you are responsible for others, you shall accept the mantle

of leadership
- Never forget - as a leader, you are always in the spotlight.
- True information is supported with strong evidence.
- Don't confuse something you have often heard as a fact. You may be a victim of an echo effect.

I just saved you a lot of time, use it like this:
- *T*here is no **SECRET** to leadership, so stop searching for it!
- A leader must earn trust first.
- Question your premise - if your actions are not giving you your desired results, check your basic assumptions.
- Here is the gold standard test - ask yourself if the list or secret will "predict failure or success?"
- We both know we won't stop looking at lists, we are people. So here is what I do, I make it a game:
    o   First, I recognize the irony of using a list to criticize lists.
    o   I assume the list will not solve anything.
    o   Evaluate the author for experience and intent. Do they want to promote themselves or help me?
    o   Identify and categorize the elements of the lists: Are they separate skills I can work on?
    o   Are the list items too general to functionally apply?
    o   Is the list just an opinion? Or, is there a study to back it up?
    o   If there is a study, what is the strength of the evidence? Is the study is empirical, observational, or anecdotal? Are the conclusions coherent within the limits of the evidence?

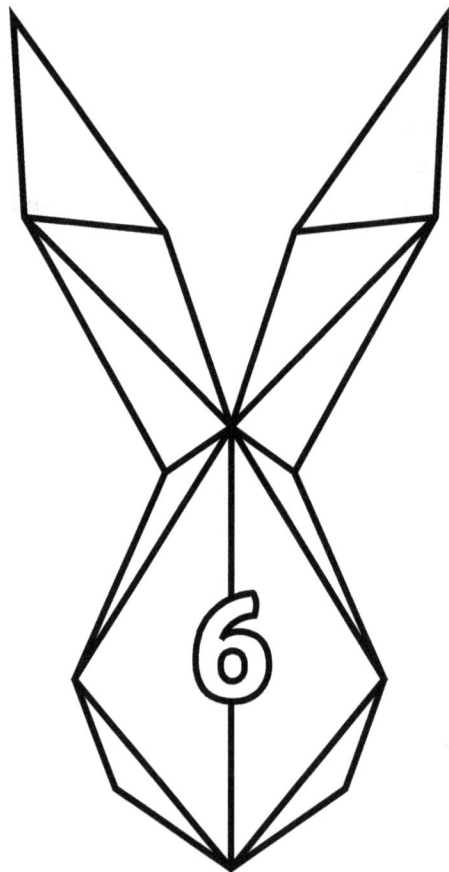

*"Integrity is doing the right thing,
even when no one is watching.*
~ C. S. Lewis

Chapter 6: "Power... is a curious thing."

Rabbit Hole 3:
*"I am in charge, I know best.
So it is my way or the highway."*

Ok, actually it is the "Power of love is a curious thing..." at least according to Huey Lewis and the News. But, power and leadership are pretty curious too.

How do you respond when your boss says "because I said so"? Is that even a legitimate comment? Are there circumstances when it is appropriate?

The tragic misunderstanding of power and leadership is that people conflate leadership with power.

My mom was a nuclear power

I remember as a kid that my mom's nuclear option was the phrase "because I said so." That phrase was the end, and there was no further discussion.

That phrase was my first recollection of what I recognize now as power.

As a kid, you fall under the social and legal umbrella of guardianship that is parenthood. You surrender to the authority of another person. It is a cultivated social behavior to yield control to authority figures. You may hate it, but it is the reality of how society functions. You have few rights until you reach the age of majority, 18 years old in the USA. Assuming your parents were not negligent or criminal in their treatment of you, you were under their control and power. Anything after 18 years old is voluntary, and you may concede authority to your parents or another person out of habit, convenience, or for financial reasons (school tuition).

For some, power is their hammer and every subordinate relationship and leadership situation are nails. There is a milestone of professional maturity that everyone, hopefully, reaches when they learn that their authority is not automatic and not absolute.

Power mongering is not leadership.

Power is more often a tool wielded to force a change in behavior or to achieve a mission, at whatever cost. If you focus on the power aspect of your position, you will be focusing on yourself. The best way to view your leadership role is that you are the steward of your organization. My concept of "good" leadership mandates an approach where the interests of the organization is the ultimate priority.

Not Leadership!!

So, what got me started on this whole topic of power and leadership; and why is it important to any of us?

There's this hyperlink that's been going around LinkedIn and the Harvard Business Review since, the earliest I could find, 2013. I'm not going to link to it because I'm tired of seeing it in my newsfeed, and I refuse to promulgate it to anyone else. The question posed is "How do you define power in one or two words?" As of January 2016, there have been over 17,000 responses... mostly with people saying whatever Wikipedia says or what sounded like something they heard in their business school classes.

But, every time I read it, I shout in my brain my two words: "Not leadership!" The trap of the ridiculous question is the implied, unspoken premise that power is the priority.

Let's take an opportunity to examine the relationship of leadership with power and the often post hoc, self-serving narrative people use to justify the misuse of power. I contend that good leadership, though harder, is the best behavior in the long run.

This might get a bit academic, buckle up.

So what does the scholarship say?

Not surprisingly, power exists on a spectrum of control between simple influence to complete control:

> *"Power is the capacity to influence another person or group to accept one's own ideas or plans."*[3]

Power is a dynamic social interaction as defined by social psychologists John R. P. French and Bertram Raven:

> *"The key to understanding power is to understand the relationship of the power holder to the person over whom the power is used, called the A (power) – B (the influenced). First, A must have some form of power. But, in order for the power to be effective, B must recognize and accept the quality of A's power."*

My operational definition of leadership is very close to the definition of power:

Leadership is a confluence of two social roles.

- The follower voluntarily surrenders to some authority (a power source as defined above).
- The leader voluntarily fills the vacuum and assumes ethical and accountable authority over a follower.

---

[3]   *"Power and Organization Development," Larry E. Greiner and Virginia Schein, Addison-Wesley Publishing, 1988*

- The leaders' loyalty is to the benefit of the organization and not to themselves.

Two important keys to my definition of leadership is that all parties are volunteering for their roles, and the purpose of all actions are in service to the health and benefit of the organization.

Sources of power

Everyone has had the experience of a person who has exercised absolute power at some point in their lives: a parent, a teacher in school, in the military, a friend, or a medical professional. My experience, in general, is that most people are responsible and fair with their power, but some abuse their power. It may not be in an immoral or criminal way, but you probably felt coerced or that you had no choice in your actions. So, what was the source of this power?

In a 1959 study by social psychologists John R. P. French and Bertram Raven, power was divided into 5 forms (later to 6 forms).

We can endlessly discuss the completeness or nuances of the list, but it is a useful embarkation point for discussion.

The list is:

1. Coercion
2. Reward
3. Legitimacy
4. Expert
5. Referent
6. Informational

Coercion is A's use of force to influence or change B's behavior. If you think back to that jerk-boss that everyone has had, the primary tool was coercion. In their mind, they were "keeping everyone on their toes." That boss uses the stick to threaten, prod, or hit. The only question is how much abuse will everyone take?

At the extreme end of coercive power, you'll find dictators. A dictator's stick isn't a monetary fine or public ridicule, but torture or even death. The people have no option to leave.

Reward is A's authority to reward B's behavior.

The reward power system can include a physical or monetary award. But more subtly, it can also include the gatekeepers who can open (or hide) opportunities.

A more socially acceptable mechanism might be in the form of a mentor.

Legitimacy is also known as "positional authority".

In my opinion, it is the most common understanding of power in business. The position of a person in an organization defines the legitimate power and the authority that is delegated to the person in the position. Accoutrements of power may also be associated with the authority: the big corner office, uniforms, robes, medals, etc.

Company executives often have a legal authority in conjunction with their position as they have a fiduciary responsibility to the shareholders.

Expert power is associated with a person's skills or special or technical knowledge that gives better insight, understanding, and judgment.

A corporate tax lawyer or architect would be good examples. Power of the expert encompasses not only the specialized abilities, but the amount of effort, time, and money to acquire the high level of skill or knowledge.

Referent is the ability to attract and hold loyal followers.

The ability could be based on charisma, interpersonal skills, or an ideology that compels its followers. The extreme negative example are cult leaders. The charisma pulls followers in, but like the Hotel California, people can come in, but the cult ideology makes it difficult to leave. The cult traits include early and complete group acceptance (a carrot for the disenfranchised), heavy social pressure to conform, complete surrender to the authority, and isolation from outside social contact and information.

Informational is A's control over B's knowledge of critical or scarce information.

The power is transitive and the power is lost once the information is provided.

In the Netherlands, there are cultural influences from the former colony of Indonesia. Examples exist in the food culture and vocabulary. You'll sometimes see the Indonesian word "toko" which translates as "store." Dutch people may apply it to mean territory – "This is my toko" meaning area of responsibility.

From this background, I often witnessed a behavior I termed "tokoism." Europe, in general, has very generous vacation policies. An employee can conceivably be out of the office for 3 to 6 weeks of vacation. In my experience it was rare to find employees cross-trained into other jobs as back-ups or for the purpose of redundancy. Absent employees normally locked up their files or kept key institutional knowledge locked up behind a password protected directory. Information critical to an employee's function would be unavailable to anyone else until the employee's return. Nobody could get into their toko unless they were there. I found it to be a disliked, but socially tolerated practice viewed as a form of job security.

It ain't the same thing!

The most important point to bear in mind is that leadership and power are not synonymous. Leadership as a subset of power, so my view is that leadership is a way of expressing power. The differentiation between power and leadership stems from the motivation of the power broker.

Power is boundless and does not account for any considera-ations besides that of the power monger, so power can be self-serving.

Ask: is power used in the best interests of the organization? Is the goal of the empowered self-oriented or work related? [4]

How do we keep the power abuse in check?

There are two important safeguards that prevent or mitigate power abuses: transparency and accountability. If you look back and examine your experience with a terrible boss, their tactics were to generally limit transparency and convince the subordinates that they, the boss-jerk, were the **final** authority

No place to hide.

Transparency is an important feature of leadership because all stakeholders will always want to confirm that everything is done in a fair manner. For example, leadership power derived from the punishment (coercion), reward, or access to information can be acceptable if the process is perceived to be consistent, fair, and judicious. When that transparency is absent, the wedge of leadership malfeasance has the chance to gain purchase.

Side effects of transparency include impressions of honesty, openness, open communications, inclusiveness, and trust - all good leadership qualities. Transparency is a specific strategy that results in qualities that lead to a strong and healthy organization. As a leader, you must construct a transparent environment.

Before anyone sends me a note...

Yes, there are some legitimate reasons for keeping information secret.

Yes, there are sometimes privacy issues, both formal and informal, that should be held closely.

Yes, there are legitimate trade secrets and intellectual property that many companies should keep secret and out of general knowledge.

4   *"Power and Organization Development," Larry E. Greiner and Virginia Schein, Addison-Wesley Publishing, 1988*

Owning it

The second important feature of leadership is accountability. Accountability is derived from several sources: social mores, ethical considerations, legal or regulatory injunctions, or censure from higher levels of authority (senior executives, boards, shareholders, etc.).

Accountability creates a workplace that manages everyone's expectations and responsibilities. By taking into account and anticipating conflicts, accountability drives an organization to be foundationally honest. In other words, a proactive philosophy of accountability creates an overarching integrity that permeates the organizational culture.

Make integrity easy and automatic.

Integrity is sometimes described as doing the right thing when nobody else is watching.

People are not by default dishonest, but they are often lazy. They may travel the low road if they think nobody is watching, or they won't get caught. Their laziness becomes culpability if their inaction breaks a rule or becomes a crime.

Systemic transparency and accountability creates an atmosphere of open communication because secrecy will not be condoned. If open and honest communication is the easiest thing, then people will follow that behavior.

As an example, dictators and cults will specifically disrupt transparency and accountability to legitimize their personal agendas. Transparency is defeated by sequestering the population from outside information that would otherwise refute the source of the cult's power. Dictators and cult leaders preemptively claim that there exists no higher levels of authority than theirs as decreed through divine rights of rule, divine providence, lineage, or raw violence. In other words, object and you can suffer eternally; if that is not enough, object and you can die.

Placing leadership above power

We cannot avoid the fact that leadership is part of the power game. I always press on specific definitions in leadership. In the absence of a definition, everyone accepts a sloppy application of power as leadership regardless of the ethical consideration or long-term destruction (value, morale, continuity, etc.). That definition includes a mutually voluntary participation from all parties and the ethical obligation that it is in everyone's best interest to work toward a healthy organizational culture.

For your consideration
- Leadership and power are inseparable. But, that does not excuse or condone power abuses.
- We are conditioned from an early age to surrender automatically to authority figures. The social reflex to surrender is the basis of the leader - subordinate relationship; it is also the basis for abuses of power.
- Never confuse overt power as leadership.
- Leadership focuses on the benefit of the organization.
- Power focuses on the benefit to the holder of power. Be wary of the self-serving narrative that says the benefit to the person with power is also to the benefit to the organization.
- Leadership is a nuanced application of power. Both leaders and followers are voluntary participants.
- Transparency and accountability are the defenses against power abuses.
- Unfortunately, people can be lazy. Make integrity a systemic feature. It manages everyone's expectations and sets the standard in support of integrity.
- Accept leadership, reject power abuses.
- Put it in terms of your own experience; how much did you hate going to work each day when you had an unreasonable boss?

I just saved you a lot of time, use it like this:
- Leadership is based on the authority of position, be it legal or social.
- There are legitimate reasons for people to hold power in an organization. There is a lot of detail above in describing the sources of power. But, it is described so that you can recognize when you see and, more importantly, know when someone is abusing that power.
- Call attention to the abuse of power, but there are some caveats.
  Caveats for your professional survival:
  1. You need to understand your own power situation in the organization - you could get fired.
  2. The basis of the power may stem from the fact that there is one person for a very specific function.
  3. Management might not know or care about fixing the abuse. (Maybe send them this book, just a suggestion.)
  4. Looking for another job is an option.
- Responsible, deliberate leadership is the best strategy for dealing with people in any organization. But, the accumulation of power and how it is used cannot be ignored. Organizational power is like electricity and needs to be understood by its users. It can be a great source of progress, or it can cause great injury. Leadership is like an insulated electrical wire. The wire routes the power to where and when it is needed. The insulation protects people and capital from potential harm or destruction.
- As leaders, we need to be vigilant for the covert accumulation of power and prevent self-serving abuses by our subordinates.
- It is through the combination of transparency and accountability that we obstruct power corruption.

- Everyone should be alert for and intolerant to blatant power abuse.
- Clearly communicate that it is unacceptable and hold abusers accountable.

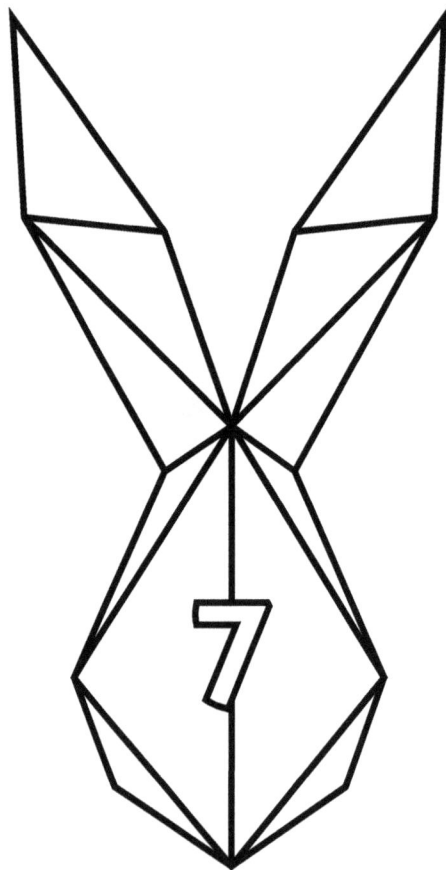

> *"The formulation of the problem is often more essential than its solution..."*
>
> ~ *Albert Einstein*

Chapter 7: Counting versus Culture

Rabbit Hole 4:
Managers are leaders.

The most common leadership argument/discussion I experience is the squabble over the definition of leadership. It is probably a sad comment on my life that leadership is discussed to the point of argument, but that is the world I occupy.

When I was in the Army, everything was leadership. I mean everything. If one of your soldiers failed, it was a failure in leadership. If you lost something or if someone you could not control directly lost something, it was a failure in leadership.

Taking responsibility and accountability was important. After all, we armed our employees. But, when everything is categorized as only one thing, it is impossible to address causality and create solutions.

The right kind of running

Running is a good analogy.

Everybody understands what running is by the definition of not walking. I know it when I see it.

But, there is actually a technical definition of running that states running is moving both legs more rapidly than walking in such a manner that during the stride, both feet are off the ground.

Ok, that is the clear meaning of running. Let's take it a step (pun intended) further. Although both are running, there is nothing the same about how you would train for a marathon versus how you would train for a 100-meter sprint. Mechanically, the movements are fundamentally the same. After that, every aspect is different.

If you wanted to optimize your performance as a sprinter, you would train completely different than if you were training as a long distance runner. You train to adapt your body to develop different types of muscle fibers.

For example, did you ever notice that at the end of a race, world class sprinters are huffing in order to catch their breath? It isn't just the exertion. It is the fact that during the 9-10 second run, they were barely breathing; almost holding their breath. Sprinters use fast-twitch, anaerobic muscles fibers in sprinting that give explosive power for a very short time.

On the other hand, world class marathon runners train to emphasize the development of slow-twitch, aerobic muscles fibers that require oxygen for endurance. This kind of muscle is highly efficient in energy conversion over a long period.

You can see the difference in how their body types are specialized for function: world class sprinters are tall and muscled for power and marathoners are smaller and thinner for endurance. Each one would dominate the other in their specialty.

Such a similar mindset is necessary for leadership and management development. For practical reasons, there is surely overlap, but the analogy holds. We identify the different needs and goals, then plan accordingly.

We have to start by defining the difference between leadership and management - sprinters and marathoners.

The Aikido Move
Aikido is one of those martial arts that might be describe as a soft martial art. The philosophy of it is to avoid the direct

clash of an attack. Instead, the attack is avoided with a lateral move and, if possible redirected.

Let's apply the same concept to managers and leaders. Instead of wasting time arguing about the accuracy of definitions, let's agree to avoid the debate completely. It is important in the discussion of leadership to differentiate between leaders and managers.

The goal is not to malign people with the title of "manager," but to distinguish the labels at an operational level that guides a clear discussion. We can use an operational definition that addresses conflicts and problems. There is no emotional investment to debate, justify, or defend; it is a definition of terms for the sake of discussion.

Leadership is a confluence of two social roles (Chapter 6).
- *The follower voluntarily surrenders to some authority (power source as defined above).*
- *The leader voluntarily fills the vacuum and assumes **ethical and accountable** authority over a follower.*
- *The leaders' loyalty is to the benefit of the organization and not to themselves.*

As the operational definition of leadership focuses on the relationship between the leader and follower, the operational definition of a manager focuses on the relationship between the manager and resources. A manager is responsible for the administration and accountability of financial, material, personnel, and time resources.

For the sake of discussion, accept the definitions as common agreement point as they is the demarcation points. In managers, you invest in reliable administration and operational continuity. In leaders, you invest in corporate culture, future leaders, a potential succession pool, and crisis management.

Leadership and management are often used as synonyms, but they are not the same concept. More simply put, management refers to resources and leadership implies a component of motivation and culture building. The more useful, common academic concepts are the terms transactional and transformational.[5]

This simple nuance allows for the segmentation of responsibilities and expectations. Many people would equate the occupancy of a management or supervisory position as being a leader. Let's agree, for the sake of a disciplined approach, that they are not the same. Leadership is not automatic element of a position, but it is a mindful application of communications, developing relationships, and influence.

Counting is the transactional part of management

I consider a "transactional leader" to be a manager. Transactional implies that there is a simple economic relationship: I give you a task, I provide the means and the resources, you perform the task, and I pay you for the task.

The proper conditions for the effective use of transactional leadership are when the tasks are highly repetitive and the need for subordinate personal interactions are low.

I have heard the comment "I pay them a fair wage, they should just shut up and do their jobs." At some level, this is a fair and appropriate comment, but if it forms the basis of your leadership style, I predict a leadership fail.

For simplicity and clarity, let's agree that the general responsibility of management is to be the steward of an organization's resources: time, money, people, and materials.

Why should you or I care?

There may be positions in a company that requires only transactional relationships. By identifying transactional positions and relationships, you can begin to delineate the

5   Bass, B. M., Avolio, B. J., & Atwater, L. E. (1996). "The transformational and transactional leadership of men and women." *Applied Psychology: An International Review 45, 5–34.*

amount of leadership training; you might begin to invest in the managers or supervisors. Too much "leadership" from well-meaning supervisors could affect the transactional process and interfere with work efficiency.

Culture comes from leaders

Transformational leadership focuses on the soft skills of human relationships and communications instead of the transactions. They are responsible for everything related to protecting the health of the organizational culture and ensuring longevity.

According to James MacGregor Burns (1978), transforming leadership is a process in which "leaders and followers help each other to advance to a higher level of morale and motivation."[6]

Bass and Riggio demonstrated in their 2006 book[7] that transformational leaders have more satisfied subordinates than non-transformational leaders.

Transformational is a means, not an end. What I mean is that each has its own domain and you shouldn't force transformational leadership into transactional situations.

For your consideration

- Management is an activity. It requires skill and expertise, and it is essential to any organization.
- Don't confuse management with leadership.
- Management functional training is not sufficient to prepare new managers for leadership challenges.
- It is unfair to everyone to expect leadership from people who have never had that leadership experience or training.

6　　*Burns, J.M, (1978), Leadership, N.Y, Harper and Row.*

7　　*"Bass, B. M., & Riggio, R. E. (2006). Transformational leadership (2nd ed.). Mahwah, NJ: Lawrence Erlbaum Associates Publishers; US.*

The company will pay in the long run with high employee turnover and disgruntled employees.

- Understand that there is a difference between management and leadership and plan accordingly.

I just saved you a lot of time, use it like this:
- Instead of arguing about leadership and management, agree on operational definitions that segment the problems and steer the conversation toward solutions.
- In a simplistic way:
  Managers protect resources.
  Leaders protect culture.
- Realize that in the real world positions may be a fusion of both. I just made a big deal out of separating leadership and management, so we could suss out and plan training and development.
- Management and leadership training must be two separate, parallel programs that address the management and leadership challenges.
- Map out career paths that, as appropriate, emphasize management skills - transition to basic leadership skills - emphasize leadership development.
- The simplest and best ways to conceptualize management is using the old functional acronym POSDCORB, which stands for the administrative processes of Planning, Organizing, Staffing, Directing, Coordinating, Reporting and Budgeting. POSDCORB has its roots in the late 1930s. Nonetheless, it summarizes, in a tidy way, the general administrative functions of management. I find it to be a great guideline for differentiating types of management training.

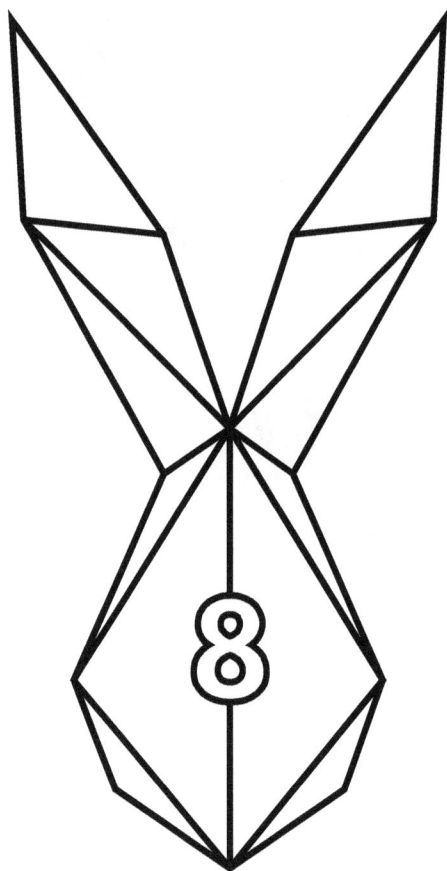

> *"Charisma is confused with so*
> *many different things that it*
> *is barely charisma anymore."*
> *~ K.W. Wrede*

Chapter 8: The Charisma Lie

Rabbit Hole 5:

The best and most inspirational leaders have charisma, and that is the most important trait a leader can have.

I had an argument with the Internet… but it actually came out ok. I didn't win and I didn't lose, but I did come away with an interesting story to share.

Leadership, like any human attribute, comes down to DNA and culture – Nature versus Nurture.

Every skill necessary to become a great leader can, unequivocally, be learned and mastered by anyone.

Full stop.

That is the "Nurture" part.

The skills and the theory represent a defined field of knowledge that can be mastered. With the proper structuring and the opportunity to develop experience, any person can become a leader. Leadership is not limited to the workplace, it can include social groups or volunteer organizations; anyplace where the common goals and a healthy culture need to be structured.

Here's where "Nature" kicks in…

If you ever saw me play basketball, you'd watch with your eyes wide open and your jaw dropped in wonder… You'd be wondering, "Is he really that bad or is he just clowning around?" No matter how much nurture I get, I'll never overcome my terrible basketball DNA.

There is one other Nature trait that is critical to becoming a leader, and it requires a very hard, and honest self-evaluation - do you really want to be the leader? Some people shun the spotlight or have no interest in guiding others. This is a completely fair and personal decision. However, it requires a strategic view of one's career path. If career progression requires leadership roles, you must either choose to accept the challenge and become the best possible leader or navigate your career into specialized, knowledge-based positions.

Recognize the potential obstacle.

The Internet discussion began…
… with a comment from a person with the initials RS.
RS:

> *"I believe Steve Cove<sic> touched upon this area of personality vs character. Great leaders focus less on styles and more on true character that creates a charisma to influence people. Persons like Gandhi, Nelson Mandela, Mother Teresa, John F Kennedy are best examples of true leaders."*

So begins the interesting story…

The original discussion between myself and RS was actually regarding leadership styles. However, his digression is a perfect example of how, as is often the case with leadership, the discussion devolves into a discussion of the ephemeral topic of charisma.

In my experience, there are three kinds of people that suggest that charisma is the key (the real secret if you will) to great leadership:

- Those who are truly charismatic and can persuade you

that charisma is important.

- Those who think they are charismatic.
- Those who think they are charismatic and want to desperately prove it, but they are not.

In the minds of the latter two, it is the fault of others for not recognizing their obvious greatness.

I fully agree that there exist people in the world who wield influence with what can be described as charisma. But, the perception of charisma is often confused with power. People are willing to surrender authority to others who occupy a particular position of power.

What is the science behind charisma (power actually)?

In the academic study of power, charisma falls under a subset of power called "Referent." Referent is defined as the ability to attract and hold loyal followers, an ability based on charisma, interpersonal skills, or an ideology that compels its followers.

As a reminder from a previous chapter, social psychologists John R. P. French and Bertram Raven, divided power into 6 categories: Coercion, Reward, Legitimacy, Expert, Referent, and Informational.

Of the categories, referent power is the only source of power that greatly depends on the psychological and social control of the relationship with the follower. It is this similarity to leadership that is the source of confusion between charisma and leadership.

To complicate the issue even more, many people confuse charisma with symbols of power such as: wealth, celebrity, or a position of authority. Our tendency to surrender authority has been key to our survival over the last 5 million years. However, the wet-wiring of our brains can betray us; make us vulnerable to manipulation.

Damn those Kardashians!!

But naturally!

As a species, we have developed a complex process of social development that has led us through those five million years of survival. On a subconscious level, we respond to non-verbal cues and symbols of power.

But power is not leadership. We have to use that big, new (realtively) 200,000 year-old part of the brain to overcome the evolutionary inertia of 5 million years.

Power is a sort of side effect of our species' long-term survival strategy - large bio mass. I covered this in an earlier chapter.

In a conflict between similar size individuals, speed and strength will generally determine the outcome. In a conflict between similar individuals, one large and one small, the large will probably win. But, add growing number of smaller adversaries and they can eventually overwhelm the larger individual - biomass is the key trait.

In a conflict between two similar size groups (equal biomass), the victor will be the group with the better ability to organize - the keys are communications and cooperation.

In the long run, as societies develop, people who can foster communication and cooperation become valued by the others as the best potential leaders

As society developed, so has legal and ethical systems that make power abuses unacceptable or, in the worst case, illegal.

As business leaders, we must have the voluntary cooperation of our followers. Without it on the individual scale, involuntary followers lead to employee turnover. On the larger social scale, involuntary followers lead to revolution or mutiny.

This is all science-y

Yes, it is all science-y, but the arguments are to point out that the study and the history of power in general, and leadership specifically, show that the relationship between leaders and followers are due to a complex, long-term evolution of the interactions between the individuals and their societies. So, when someone argues that the basis of leadership is charisma, I can only assume that they are a bit lazy and want a short-cut.

They romanticize charisma, overestimate their qualities of charisma, and oversell the virtues of charisma. What they secretly covet is the power. Leadership is too much hard work.

They want to cultivate a referent power base that they will use for their own gain or glory. They hope to rely only on their own charisma, their interpersonal skills, or some underlying ideology to influence other people. The subtle nature of this manipulation makes it difficult to defend against.

The best metric to test if the leader is sincere is to ask the question: who benefits, the group or the person controlling the group?

Can you handle the truth?

The best way to uncover the truth about charisma is to put it in true context. RS referred to Gandhi, Nelson Mandela, Mother Teresa, and John F. Kennedy in his discussion. He described them as charismatic, but in actuality, they were purveyors of their own specific ideologies - thought leaders. They were compelling because of the timing and power of their messages. From the academic point of view, their power was based on a referent combination of charisma and ideologies.

From an academic view, charisma is the thinnest veil of power - an academic sub-category (charisma) of a power category (referent). If people do not (or cannot) perceive your charisma, what is your leadership foundation?

Charisma, I Reject Thee!!

If you have charisma, it can be a fantastic leadership tool. But, can you truly depend on it? What happens when your winning smile and charming personality are not enough in a crisis situation or a period of continuing crisis?

I have several reasons for rejecting the magical thinking of charisma, and they are not what you might normally consider. As any EndGame Leadership discussion should include, it is about the long-term survival of an organization.

First, charisma is not a predictor of success. Conversely, the absence of charisma is not a predictor of failure.

I have not read a single study or article that ever traced back the failure of a company or organization to charisma. I have never heard of any company or organization that traced their success solely to charisma. There have been unlikeable people who succeeded and wonderful people with loyal followers who failed.

Starting with a little common sense, let us pretend for a moment that charisma was the reason that Steve Jobs, Elon Musk, and Jack Welch turned their companies into the powerhouses of each of their industries. Take it a step further and stipulate that there are another 100 US companies that are succeeding for the same reasons.

103 businesses - these companies are the outliers.

A 2013 study from the US Census Bureau stated that there are about 1,575 large companies (1500+ employees) and about 5.85 million medium-sized companies (101-1499 employees) in the US. It makes a lot more sense to study the successes of those 5.851575 million companies (precision is compelling) than to study the small sample of 103 - or .00001706%.

Charisma as not a reliable leadership skill. Charisma as a leadership trait is overrated and glamorized in popular literature and popular media. The effect of the inflated value reveals itself as two-sides of the same coin.

The first side is the overinflated opinion of those who self-report their amazing charisma. Strong self-confidence is an important aspect of leadership communications skills, but some people take self-confidence to an irrational level. Sometimes, their perception of their own charisma borders on delusion. Leaders who cannot honestly self-assess are a danger to themselves, their employees, and their organizations.

The flip-side of the coin is that many people are persuaded by the media that charisma is a prerequisite to becoming a leader. They do not picture themselves as charismatic and thereby preemptively disqualify themselves. So, the very people with the ability to look at themselves honestly and assess their qualities, dismiss themselves as qualified leaders. They dismiss themselves based on a pseudo-metric that is not a predictor of success.

My final rejection of charisma is this simple statement: charisma is not a teachable skill. Neither the studies of leadership theory or management theory wastes a single second on charisma training because it is not a measurable, tangible quality.

Charisma may be the first impression we have of people, but it is not what keeps employees around for the long-term or in times of trouble.

For your consideration
- Charisma is not the foundation of leadership.
- Charisma is not a predictor of success or failure.
- Don't waste time arguing on the Internet.
- Leadership can be taught; charisma cannot.
- Leadership is a voluntary role. If you do not enjoy the role, there is no shame in seeking another pathway.
- Some people have charisma and that is a useful tool, but it is not a prerequisite of leadership.
- Charisma is not power; charisma is a minor aspect of power.
- Recognize when you are being manipulated. We have evolved to respond to power in its different forms at an unconscious level. When you recognize the manipulation, it is then your choice.
- Do not confuse charisma with a compelling story or ideology.

- Charisma is self-reported and prone to biases, both positive and negative.

I just saved you a lot of time, use it like this:
Managers supervise, leaders guide - My best bosses were not always the most charismatic people in the world. But, they always supported and encouraged me. They taught me, guided me away from big problems, and tolerated my mistakes on the small things.

- Earn Loyalty - Those great bosses earned a stronger, more valuable, and more lasting commodity than my temporary admiration of their charisma - they had my loyalty.
- There are skills that others confuse with charisma, work on those skills.

  A friend of mine would argue that charisma can be taught. I would say that he confuses charisma with strong communications skills. Now, those are skills that can be taught!

  If others confuse those skills with charisma, that is your luck, but don't fool yourself.

  I suggest two goals:
  - Hone your communications skills and become an interesting, compelling speaker.
  - Hone the other side of communications and become an active listener.
- Take the long view and create a corporate environment that leads to a healthy organizational culture. A healthy culture will generate loyalty, innovation, and sustain the organization in times of crisis.

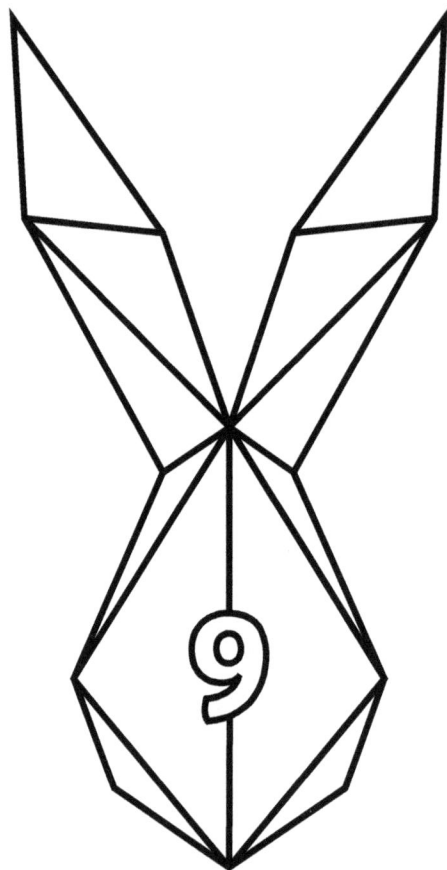

*"A false premise is an incorrect
proposition that forms the basis
of an argument or syllogism."*

~ **Wikipedia, the free encyclopedia**

Chapter 9: The Style Trap

Rabbit Hole 6:
*You are your leadership style, and your leadership style is you.
"We know he is hard on the employees, but he'll never change.
And, anyway, he gets results."*

Leadership style is one of those conversations that almost always leads to a lot of confusion. The conversation often begins with the question "Which style is best?"

The question itself is based on two false premises that form the upper and lower jaws of the style trap. These two assumptions are the two most critical, egregious mistakes in the approach of leadership style.

The first critical mistake is the assumption that leadership style is related to personality. The second critical mistake is the assumption that leadership style is fixed and, like your personality, cannot easily be changed.

It begins with passive acceptance.

It seems normal to our bottom-up experience that leadership development begins with understanding ourselves better. It makes sense. It feels natural.

So, it is common for everyone to take leadership and personality assessments as a means of measuring personalities and leadership potential. Almost 90% of Fortune 100 companies perform these tests. The ubiquity of these assessments and their universal acceptance has created a widely recognized conclusion that leadership and personality type are mutually entangled.

I make the argument that leadership and personality types are mutually exclusive items, so the importance of assessments relies on a false premise.

We accept it because it seems like science

Assessments seem compelling because they are casually accepted by everyone without questions - from HR professionals to leadership trainers to senior executives. I suspect that they have all been exposed to personality assessments throughout their professional lives and they assume the tests to be valid. We have been conditioned to accept the results of these assessments because they physically resemble other standardized tests that we have taken throughout our lives: SATs, ACTs, GMATs, ASVABs.

It becomes a foregone requirement for many companies to use assessment testing in the recruiting process.

But, who questions the validity of the assessments?

I have taken these assessments:

- Leadership style assessments: are you a democratic leader, authoritarian, or somewhere in between?
- What is your personality type (FIRO-B, MBTI)?
- What is your role as a team member (Belbin)?

My first thought about the results is always, "Interesting, but so what?"

Are these useful tools?

Can we use them to predict behaviors, success, or failure?

The simple truth is that there is very little evidence that prove assessments are accurate because there are no quality studies, to my knowledge, which show those assessments can reliably predict success in groups or individuals.

Consequently, there is no way to predict the success or failure of a personality type in leadership.

The problem is that the most popular assessments are based on the most superficial, self-reported testing methods that are themselves based on weak or nonexistent science. The most reliable personality assessments are intensive interview evaluations performed by psychological professionals - a process that is too time consuming and expensive to perform on a large scale.

Enter cheap, weak, standardized testing

"Two and a half million Americans a year take the Myers-Briggs. Eighty-nine companies out of the US Fortune 100 make use of it, for recruitment and selection or to help employees understand themselves or their co-workers."[8]

At about $150-$200 per test, the Myers-Briggs Type Indicator® (MBTI®) accounts for $375-$500 million in annual revenue in the US alone.

Many popular assessments measure self-reported traits and use the results to categorize the participants. Most assessments are designed based on post hoc results, results that are rationalized after a specific outcome has occurred.

For instance, let's say I wanted to study the top four personality traits of a group of people that I call "successful leaders." Assume I evaluated 1000 leaders and found that each of the top four traits occurs 25% of the time. It would be statistically conceivable that my top four traits may not overlap in any of my respondents. Consequently, if I tested later candidates and wanted good candidates to have two or more traits, I might find that nobody has more than one.

The results of the tests are weak for two reasons. First, the results can vary over time. It seems pretty unscientific to assume

8   http://www.psychometric-success.com/personality-tests/personality-tests-popular-tests.htm

anyone will have significant personality changes from one month to another. Reliability, consistency, and replication are important characteristics of any science. The second weakness is predictability.

The tests may claim to accurately categorize people, it is no accident that the assessments make no recommendations or predictions.

They have none to make.

I recently took a behavior analysis assessment online. I think it was only about 25 questions. I answered the questions honestly and came out as a middle of the road leader who should be a consultant - Ok, no surprise.
My professional philosophy on building healthy organizational culture conflicts with the stereotype "winner-take-all" leader.

I could tell by the timbre of the questions that the testers had some preconceived stereotypes related to individual, team, and leadership characteristics and behavior. I could have easily gamed the result. I could tell that their criteria for leadership would have been a meticulous, mission-first, organization man. A stereotype based on popular myth, not science.

For these reasons, the validity of many popular, mainstream assessments are challenged by psychological professionals.[9]

The house of cards collapses

I want to craft an amazing series of arguments and chain of logic that proves that leadership is not your personality.

But, pfffft… I don't have to.

The original premise was that personality traits were the keys to predicting good leaders, but the current, most popular tools on the market clearly cannot properly evaluate personalities or roles. Hence, if the foundation collapses, the style question collapses too.

You are not your style.

---

9   *http://www.denverpost.com/lifestyles/ci_22210169/myers-briggs-personality-test-embraced-by-employers-not*

Style doesn't control you; you control it

The biggest problem in accepting that there is one perfect style is that by labeling yourself, you eliminate your other options. Let's flip the conversation around and start with new assumptions.

First, you are you.

Second, you have a certain skill set.

Third, you are a sum of your personality and experience.

If something happens at the office that requires your leadership authority - where do you start?

In some ways, leadership style is like a suit. You make daily fashion style choices appropriate to specific occasions: formal wear for galas, business attire for meetings, casual fashion for a first date, and large foam hands for sporting events. The best selection is the proper fit for each occasion.

Another way to view leadership style as a functional toolset. A single leadership style is not suitable for every occasion; the trick is to know when to be a hard-ass and when to take the time to be wholly democratic. One of my favorite references is Daniel Goleman's "Leadership That Gets Results" (Harvard Business Review March–April 2000 Issue.)

Goleman defines six styles of leadership:
- Coercive
- Authoritarian
- Affiliative
- Democratic
- Pacesetting
- Coaching

We can discuss all day the completeness of Goleman's classifications, but we are building a leadership model. If the model fits your world, use it.

Feel free to modify on your own, but let this version be your springboard.

In broad terms, each style is a measurement of how much

participation the followers have in any decision processes. With a coercive style, followers have no power or decision authority. At the opposite end, decision authority is shared with subordinates in a democratic style. In fact, the underlying agreement is that the decision will not be vetoed by the boss.

The application of the style is not left to the capricious nature (personality) of the leader, but the style is determined by the circumstances of resources.

No style is always the right style

Each leadership style is more effective than another under differing circumstances. In fact, circumstances are key to choosing the proper style. The style is determined by the availability of resources - time is usually the most critical resource.

The democratic style is most effective if there is time for discussion. Democratic decisions can create a sense of involvement and inclusion for the group that contributes to cohesion.

A coercive leadership style is sometimes necessary when time is critical. The less time there is available, the greater the urgency.

In an emergency, it may be necessary to tell people what to do (coerce or exert authority). Immediate action is urgently required, so there is little chance to communicate or explain, because time is key. In non-crisis periods, if you rely on coercion to implement common daily tasks, people will perceive the injustice and, eventually, resist cooperation. In the long-term, and if they can, employees in a coercive environment will leave as soon as it is practical.

Coercive leadership is acceptable in crisis. Like a crisis, coercion should be the exception, not the norm. An authoritarian style can be effective during emergencies in a healthy organizational culture. The group will trust that leaders are acting to resolve the crisis and are doing it for the benefit of the group. Also, once the crisis has passed, the circumstances and reason why decisions were made can be reviewed and explained to everyone.

Just a quick side note here. If your workplace is a chaotic fur ball or a series of crises to manage and fires to put out, then a coercive or overly authoritarian style may be a symptom of poor processes or organization.

The story of my style

I am by nature an affiliative leader; I know that about myself without an assessment. My preference is to build team cohesion and minimize conflict. My biggest mistakes in my earlier leadership roles was to assume that since my nature was affiliative, it meant I always had to be the peacemaker. I often, somehow, tried to force everything into the affiliative paradigm which was not always successful. Even though I may have been technically successful, perhaps I was not optimally successful at the risk of some intangible cost.

For example, in those early days, I was not comfortable or confident with confrontation. As a result, I am sure that some people perceived my leadership style as too soft.

They were right.

It made later interactions unnecessarily difficult. I eventually learned how to both deal with confrontation and how to be confrontational, or more authoritative.

I still prefer cooperation and affiliation, but they are not a requirement for every situation. I have been lucky because according to Goleman, affiliative leadership is the best way to run the leadership marathon. It is simply good culture building.

By contrast, one of my best friends is a Command Sargent Major in the US Marine Corps, Spencer E. Scott. Unsurprisingly, he has one the most authoritarian leadership styles of anyone I know. From an organizational culture point of view, this is not a surprise.

The one reason he has been successful is that in his authoritarian role there is no doubt in anyone's mind that everything he does is in service to his group of people in this order: his Marines, his unit, parent unit, the Marine Corps. Excluding mandatory privacy requirements, no punishment or reward is performed in secret. There is a transparency, including a right to counsel, that is evident to everyone. The transparency reinforces culture, and positive and negative behavior.

In the execution of his authoritarian style, he is always transparent, consistent, fair, and self-correcting.

However, the most important aspect of his style is that he does not ignore the use of the other leadership styles. He is affiliative, democratic, and a coach whenever he needs to use those roles. So, contrary to the culture or surface appearance from an outsider's point of view, the key to his success has been his mastery of the complete tool set of leadership styles.

The notion of a single leadership style is a trap that limits your ability to lead effectively. Apply yourself to understand the different leadership styles and when to use them.

A final trap: the communication misconception

There is a common mistake made by both leaders and followers. It is a nuance of leadership that I think is worthy of a bit of discussion. Many people confuse leadership style with communications style. By parsing out the two different elements, it gives us a chance to analyze and correct real and potential problems.

We have covered the first part in some detail already in this chapter. We have defined leadership style as the way you share decision authority with subordinates or followers. Troubleshooting style relies on applying the appropriate style to each situation.

The second part seems the same on the surface, and that is why there is confusion. The second part is your communication style.

Communications styles and skills are a completely different subject from leadership. They are very, very important to good leadership, and they are tightly connected, but should not be confused with leadership.

The point I am making is that as you are building up a healthy corporate culture and as you exercise the appropriate leadership styles, your subordinates will judge your leadership abilities along with your communications skills.

In service to the EndGame Leadership model, you must view leadership style and communications style as two separate functions. Leadership style is a situational response. Communications style is how you frame the message and express the leadership response to everyone else.

Leadership style is one set of problems and solutions.

Communications style is a completely separate set of problems and solutions.

If you are perfectly executing every leadership style in the proper circumstances, but subordinates do not think you listen or if you speak in a gruff or terse way, you lose much of the advantage and effects of appropriate leadership styles.

Separate out those two parts and you now understand which skill sets need your attention. For example, if you are a new leader, and you are nervous speaking with people, you may unintentionally avoid or minimize conversation. You may believe in Goleman's different styles, but the perception of the employees may be that you are removed or don't care.

You want to be a good leader and you want to effectively and correctly express your ideas, thoughts, and objectives to your subordinates in the best way possible. You must develop communications skills as a part of your leadership toolbox.

Don't allow fear to rule your leadership style.

A final study

According to 2014 McKinsey review:

- Two-thirds of 500 executives polled listed leadership as their number one human capital concern.

- Only 7% of executives believe that their company develops leaders effectively.

There is obviously a gaping chasm between the goal and the execution. Hundreds of millions of dollars are spent each year on personality testing. Senior executives are still concerned about human capital in general and in leadership development specifically.

The primary problem is that the execution of the goal is based on the wrong premise. It is a waste of time and effort to measure personalities of potential employees. A better use of the money is in developing effective leadership programs to manage the employees. Train the leaders to engage more effectively and motivate their portion of the organization's human capital. Give them the correct tools and training on when to use them.

For your consideration

- People who cling to the idea that their single leadership style is tied to their personality will use that excuse as a reason not to change.
  Further, it will be their excuse for their bad behavior and the bad behavior of subordinates.
  That behavior is a threat to your organization.
  You have already met them, but excused them too. Now you know better.
- Personality assessments can be gamed.
- Many assessments are rejected by psychological professionals.
- Leadership style is not an inherent personality characteristic.
- Leadership style is not "one size fits all."
- Assessments are not reliable tests of leadership style.
- Asking what personality trait makes a better leader is like asking what personality makes a better golfer.
  It is a non sequitur.
  A good golfer, like a good leader, selects the right tool at the right time and uses it in the most effective manner.

- Choose the right leadership style for the circumstances.
- There is a gap between the strategic importance companies place on leadership and its execution.

I just saved you a lot of time, use it like this:

- Wipe from your mind the idea that your personality determines your leadership style.
  The label of a single style limits ou.
- Every time you see an article that speaks to leadership and personality relationships - laugh in derision!
  Ha! Haaaaa!
- There are two personality traits that will affect your capability to lead:
  1. Fear
  2. Your ability to deal with risk
  If they affect you, they are separate issues that you need to address.
- If there was one bit of insight I wish I had at the beginning of my career, it would have been the structure and categorization of Goleman's leadership styles. Study Goleman's approach and understand the drivers behind the styles and you will have a better, and more effective tool set.
- There is nothing more useful and valuable that you can begin to use right now, than understanding the relationships between the different Goleman styles.
- Stop focusing on assessments.
- Assessments do not define a leader.
- Caveats:
  I have two assessment exceptions:
  The first is the occasional 360 review. 360s are expensive and time-consuming to manage, but I think they are a great diagnostic tool when applied as a magnifying glass to smaller problem units.
  The key is the protection of input anonymity. If you really have a leadership problem, anticipate retaliation.

Second, if you have a problem executive or employee, and you feel they are worth the effort to rehabilitate, the personality assessments can be a great way to open a conversation.

It is like a polygraph test.

Polygraphs are fallible and, as evidence, are not admissible in court. But for investigators, a polygraph is a great tool. It has proven itself to be a great way to get people to open up and talk about things that they might not otherwise discuss. (Perhaps it may not be in a criminal's best interest, but the rest of the analogy is pretty solid.)

ABOUT THE AUTHOR

Ken Wrede is an experienced business executive and entrepreneur with an international, wide-ranging background in the overseas business, consulting, and startup companies. He has 27 years of cross-cultural experience in the US, South Korea, The Netherlands, Spain, and France.

He holds an EMBA from École des Hautes Études Commerciales d'Paris (HEC Paris), Paris, France (with an emphasis in innovation and entrepreneurship), an M.Sc. from the Golden Gate University (with an emphasis on telecommunications and business), and a BA from Mississippi State University in broadcast communications.

He was a founder and principle executive in four European startup companies and as a principle executive two additional startup companies. His first startup was a small boutique consulting company in the Netherlands, followed by two telecom companies in the emerging, liberalized markets of The Netherlands and Spain, and finally, he cofounded one of the earliest private incubators in Spain.

Ken writes extensively on leadership and leadership modeling. Ken writes in a blog on issues concerning leadership, business, and critical thinking: www.EndgameLeadership.com.

Ken has lived in five different countries and worked in ten. He has professional experience in a variety of industries including the military, international business, startup companies, and international security.

He attributes all the success that he has enjoyed to strong leadership principles and the development of the most important resource: people.

www.ingramcontent.com/pod-product-compliance
Lightning Source LLC
Chambersburg PA
CBHW060620200326
41521CB00007B/829